PRAYING INTO
YOUR PURPOSE

ANDREA JACKSON

Published by Ushindi Publishing:
UshindiPublishing.com
64 West Central Avenue, Suite 1138
Edgewater, MD 21037

Publishing Consultation by ELOHAI International Publishing & Media:
elohaiintl.com

Print ISBN: 979-8-9998668-0-6
Ebook ISBN: 979-8-9998668-1-3

Dedication

To my wonderful husband, children, father, mother, and siblings. Thank you for your unconditional love, support, and prayers.

Contents

INTRODUCTION

Discovering Your Divine Purpose

Prayer is one of the most powerful tools God has given us. In prayer, we can learn our purpose, gain the strength to bear it, and obtain the direction to live it. Sadly, many people journey through life without ever knowing their purpose. Operating at your full potential comes from purposeful living.

Understanding Purpose, Destiny, and Assignment

Before we go further, let's clarify three important terms you will encounter throughout this book:

Purpose: the reason for your existence; why God created you; your very being, who you are.

Destiny: your predestined future, including events and things that God has intended to occur in your life.

Assignment: specific tasks God designates you to complete.

In short, humanity's primary purpose is to worship God—to reflect His image and walk in relationship with Him. Our purpose is to serve the purposes of God. Our God-given assignment is to have dominion, be fruitful, and multiply to replenish the earth. Ultimately, our eternal destiny is heaven (Gen. 1:26-31; Ps. 86:9; 2 Cor. 5:1,8). However, distinct from God's purpose for creating humanity, He meticulously crafted a unique purpose, destiny, and specific assignments for you.

Jeremiah exemplifies God's personalized plan. Ordained as a prophet before birth, his purpose was "to root out and to pull down, to destroy and to throw down, to build and to plant" (Jer. 1:10). Throughout his ministry, God gave Jeremiah explicit assignments, such as the symbolic acts of the linen belt and the broken jar. God instructed him to buy a linen belt, hide it, and later retrieve it; then to purchase a clay jar from a potter, break it in front of the people, and proclaim God's judgment. Jeremiah's destiny was certain. The people would fight against him, but God promised to rescue him and remain with him.

From Jeremiah's life, we learn that while all humanity shares a collective purpose and destiny, each person also carries a unique, God-given calling. I encourage you to read the book of Jeremiah to discover the full scope of his mission and how it reveals God's intentional design for every life.

You Were Created to Solve a Problem

Every invention was created to solve a problem. Thomas Edison has been named one of the greatest inventors of all time. He saw the need for light and thus created the light bulb. In the presence of a necessity to reproduce sound, Edison invented the phonograph. Edison invented over 20 items and held 1,093 patents. Although he was partially deaf and his inventions had many failed attempts, we can agree that his inventions were worth pursuing, despite the numerous challenges he faced.

Here is what is important about Edison's story: he discovered his purpose by identifying a need and worked persistently to meet it. Like Edison, you were created with a specific problem in mind, a need that only you can meet in the unique way God designed you to meet it. Your purpose is not random. It is intentional. And as Edison faced obstacles, his deafness, and countless failures, you may face challenges on your journey. But those challenges do not disqualify you from your purpose; they often prepare you for it.

God, above all humanity, creation, wisdom, and the greatest power, did not create anything without purpose. He is intentional! You can spend a lifetime and eternity trying to understand the mind of God, yet you will never fully comprehend. One thing is certain: you can gain insight into your purpose and live it out to the glory of God. I am a living witness!

My Journey from Church Work to True Purpose
I have spent countless years of my life healing and unpacking trauma while working in the kingdom. I was satisfied in believing the facade that church "work" was my purpose. I have had countless opportunities to work in the church and serve citizens in the kingdom. Through my church work, I have gained much insight, developed skill sets, and gained wisdom, all of which have been beneficial to every facet of my life. Yet God called me away from the mindset that "church work" equaled my purpose. This revelation was difficult to unpack, as I grew up in the church and witnessed believers' transformation through church work. But this was not my purpose.

Prayer was the key that unlocked the door to identify and execute the purpose God intended for my life. Being prayerful is essential when seeking your purpose, as God can provide the revelation you need to fully execute assignments within it, for the sake of your destiny. Through prayer, I learned how challenges, events, trials, situations, and life lessons all played a vital role in walking in my purpose. God taught me through instruction, revelation, dreams, and visions.

What This Book Will Do for You

This book will guide you in building a purposeful life of prayer, which is the key to walking in the plan God prepared for you before the foundation of the world. By the end of this journey together, you will:

- Understand how to use prayer and Scripture to discover your purpose
- Learn practical tools to hear God's voice clearly
- Discover how to cultivate and walk in your purpose with confidence
- Recognize the difference between worldly success and Kingdom fruitfulness
- Develop the spiritual disciplines necessary to fulfill your destiny

Are you ready? Let's begin this journey of discovering and walking in the purpose God created you for.

CHAPTER ONE

The Necessity of Scripture for Your Purpose

About a year ago, the siren call of a new smartphone finally lured me in. My old phone was sputtering, its battery life dwindling faster than my patience, and the promise of upgraded features was too tempting to resist. I ventured into the bright, buzzing phone store, eager to hold a new cellular device in my palm.

The friendly associate, a tech-savvy guide in this digital jungle, patiently helped me navigate the setup process: data transfer, account activation—the whole shebang. I walked out of the store clutching my shiny new device, the box containing the user manual (all 173 pages of it!), and the little SIM card tool, feeling as though I had just leveled up in the game of life. Relief washed over me because I was long overdue for a cell phone upgrade.

For the past year, my phone has been my primary camera, map, and connection to the digital world. Yet, that hefty user manual has remained untouched, gathering dust in a drawer. Why bother wading through pages of technical jargon when I can figure things out as I go along? But the truth is, I know I am only scratching the surface. I am sure there are hidden features, clever shortcuts, and powerful tools lurking in my phone that I have yet to discover.

The camera options alone feel like a mystery waiting to be unlocked. Does this sound familiar to you?

In a similar vein, consider the Word of God. Our Creator, in His infinite wisdom, has gifted us with Scripture, a comprehensive guide for navigating life's complexities and growing into mature, well-equipped sons of God. The Bible is not merely a collection of stories; it is our user manual, God-inspired and packed with His essential instructions and prophecy. As 2 Timothy 3:16-17 (NIV) reminds us, it is "profitable for doctrine, for reproof, for correction, for instruction in righteousness, that the man of God may be complete, thoroughly equipped for every good work." Just as my phone manual holds untapped potential, so too does the Bible hold secrets to a richer, more fulfilling life. It is time to dust off that manual and unlock the fullness of what God has for us.

Getting to Know God Through Scripture

As a child, I learned the acronym of the Bible is the Basic Instructions Before Leaving Earth. I took that to heart. I read the Bible fervently, determined to absorb every word. I memorized the books in order, studied their genres, internalized stories, scriptures, characters, and more. I was relentless in my desire to know every facet of God's Word. Nothing could stop me.

As I matured, my perspective on the Bible shifted. I began utilizing the Bible to get to know God, rather than gathering biblical facts. Scripture tells us that eternal life is found in knowing God (John 17:3). Scripture is rich with intricate details about who God is. Its primary purpose is that we may know Him. Yet many overlook this, using Scripture as a means to an end rather than a path to intimacy. Who would not want to access eternal life through relationship with God? In my experience, when you begin to use Scripture and prayer as tools to know God—not just learn about

Him—He begins to trust you with mysteries and hidden truths through the revelation of His character.

Your purpose is hidden in the One who created it when He created you. As you immerse yourself in the Bible, I encourage you to set your intent on pursuing to know God, not to chase purpose, destiny, or assignments. When your heart is postured toward knowing Him, Scripture comes alive with understanding and revelation. If anything, good or bad, rises above your desire for God, it becomes idolatry. Even passion for your purpose, if greater than your desire for Him, is idolatry. God desires to be sought above all else.

Interestingly, many unbelievers extract principles from Scripture to fuel their personal success, while rejecting the God behind those principles. They apply His Word without seeking His heart. But when you apply God's principles with the intent to please Him and deepen your relationship with Him, that insight becomes truly transformative. Let your desire to know God be the driving force behind your study of Scripture.

Consider Apostle Paul. Before his conversion, he was a Pharisee— well-versed in the Torah, yet he did not know God. It was not until his encounter on the road to Damascus that his journey toward intimacy with God began. Paul had information about Jesus, but lacked relationship. After his conversion, that information became the foundation for a deep and personal relationship. In Philippians 3, Paul expresses his longing: "I want to know Christ— yes, to know the power of his resurrection and participation in his sufferings, becoming like him in his death."

So, I ask you: Are you engaging with Scripture merely to gather information about God, or are you seeking to know Him through it?

My mother once promised to take my son to Disneyland. Oh, my goodness, I heard about this Disneyland trip for days, weeks, and even months! Anything that remotely resembled Disneyland would instantly ignite my son's boundless excitement for his anticipated trip with his grandmother. It was truly never-ending! My son trusted his grandmother completely. He was filled with excitement and absolute confidence that her promise would come true. There was no plane ticket, no Disneyland pass, no packed luggage, and no set date. But he believed. Because she said it would happen, he banked on it happening with full conviction.

While reading and studying Scripture are excellent tools to get to know God, you must move beyond mere intellectual assent to truly believing what He says and hiding it in your heart. This act, as Psalm 119:11 (NIV) declares, "I have hidden your word in my heart that I might not sin against you," elevates His Word to an entirely new level of impact and power in your life. The very root of belief is trust. Therefore, cultivate and build your trust in God incrementally, day by day, through His Word, as you take Him at His Word and courageously allow what He says to operate, guide, and transform every aspect of your life.

Establishing Your Identity

You need Scripture to establish your identity as a believer. It will provide guidance as you dive into your reason for existence and begin pursuing specific, time-bound tasks. I would venture to say, without daily Scripture reading, adaptation, acceptance, and application, one will grieve their identity, purpose, destiny, and assignments. Just as your vehicle requires gasoline for motion, you require daily Scripture to proceed forward for the glory of God.

It is an immutable truth that you cannot truly operate in your God-given purpose without consistently engaging, executing, and operating in and with Scripture. Scripture is more than a collection of ancient writings; it is God's comprehensive instructions and prophetic revelation, carefully outlining His instructions, command-ments, and divine purposes. Within its sacred pages, we discover the very essence of what pleases God. We receive the foundational knowledge necessary to walk in alignment with His will.

Ultimately, one of God's supreme desires for His people is holiness, a core attribute of His nature, as emphatically declared in 1 Peter 1:16 (NIV): "Be holy, because I am holy." This divine mandate compels us to understand holiness not through human lenses, but through God's perfect standard. As defined by Webster's 1828 Dictionary, "holy" encapsulates "purity or integrity of moral character; freedom from sin; sanctity." This definition immediately highlights the absolute necessity of intimacy with God through the Holy Spirit for the achievement of God's holy mandate.

Indeed, Scripture provides explicit instructions for living a life that is not only pleasing to God but also perfectly aligned with His will. As the Psalmist beautifully declared in Psalms 119:105 (KJV), "Thy word is a lamp unto my feet, and a light unto my path." This verse shows that God's Word is our unfailing compass, and final authority. It offers more than general guidance; it reveals the specific steps we should take. Through Scripture, God provides wisdom, insight, and clear direction to help us shape every part of our lives to reflect and honor Him.

By immersing ourselves in Scripture, we gain the invaluable ability to discern God's will, empowering us to make informed decisions that are rooted in His eternal truth rather than fleeting human opinions or desires. From this Scripture, we grasp that God's Word is the very source of our direction, showing us precisely the way to go.

An important reality to accept is that mankind does not possess the inherent ability to accurately define God's standard of purity, integrity, or moral character. Our very nature is sinful, "for all have sinned and fall short of the glory of God" (Rom. 3:23 KJV). We are, in fact, born into sin, which means that any definition of purity, integrity, or moral character will originate from our unregenerated selves and inevitably be skewed and tainted. This limitation underscores the immense value, purpose, and absolute necessity of both the Holy Spirit and the Holy Scriptures. It is through the power of the Holy Spirit and the infallible truth of Scripture that we can truly define and align our lives to mirror God's holiness. Therefore, before embarking on the exploration of the specific purpose God has for your life, I fervently encourage you to first dive deep into understanding God's character, as revealed through Scripture, and commit to allowing the Holy Spirit to begin transforming your life to align with God's perfect, pure, integral, and moral character.

Establishing Your Identity with Scripture
Your identity, the core of who you are, must undergo a radical transformation by renewing your mind. As exhorted in Romans 12:2 (NIV), "Do not conform to the pattern of this world, but be transformed by the renewing of your mind. Then you will be able to test and approve what God's will is—his good, pleasing and perfect will." Your authentic identity in God is not self-conceived; it is shaped and rooted by His unblemished Word. Accepting, believing, and actively adapting your identity to what God says about you will bring you into agreement with His pronouncements and the identity He designed for your life. While this journey of transformation is undeniably a lifelong task and may at times appear tedious or challenging, please understand that it is not only beneficial but necessary for you to fulfill your purpose and complete assignments so that you can obtain your destiny.

Your self-esteem, how you perceive and value yourself, must be firmly rooted in Scripture, rather than the shifting sands of worldly opinions or personal feelings. For believers, our self-esteem is about aligning with God's perspective on what He says about us. Therefore, you cannot afford to neglect reading, studying, accepting, digesting, and consistently adapting to Scripture. How you feel about yourself profoundly impacts every single aspect of your life, influencing your intimate relationship with God and your interactions with others. Literally every facet of your life is impacted by your self-esteem: the pursuit of your purpose, setting and achievement of your goals, ambitions, and so much more.

As a life coach, I recall an impactful experience working with a marvelous young lady who possessed an abundance of potential. She had already accomplished many things, held an in-depth, inspiring vision for her future, and was fueled by immense motivation and an immeasurable sense of value for her goals. As a believer, I had the privilege of helping her overcome complacency, develop significantly in her ministry, graduate from college, establish healthy relational boundaries, improve her physical health by losing weight and adopting a healthy lifestyle, and implement a godly routine, among countless other achievements.

However, despite all this, she struggled with deeply entrenched low self-esteem and a debilitating sense of self-worth, which severely prevented her from accelerating forward and fully embracing God's magnificent purpose for her life. It was at this critical juncture that I began to relentlessly challenge her self-perspective against the irrefutable truth of Scripture. Through the power of the Holy Spirit, we pulled down the stronghold of negative self-talk and self-sabotage, empowering her to fully accept and agree with God concerning what He sovereignly said about her through

Scripture. Scripture became the foundational tool in developing her new, Christ-centered identity, systematically peeling off the layers of her old, broken self. Hallelujah, there is freedom in God's Word!

To truly walk in your ordained identity and God's purpose, you will need to dive deep into Scripture, not just for reading, but also so that you can effectively pray the Scriptures. Remember, God is holy, and because of His unchanging holiness, He is bound to keep every one of His words. His Word is Scripture, and Scripture is His Word. In fact, He puts His Word above His name. You can find security, reassurance, and ultimate peace in God's promises, knowing that His impeccable reputation speaks for itself across history and eternity. His Word never fails.

Scripture for Instruction

In my journey, I have learned an immeasurable amount about God simply by diligently reading and studying the Bible. It is truly amazing how intimately He speaks to me through His Word, consistently providing revelation and practical guidance for my life's path. Reading the Bible has become a daily regimen, a spiritual sustenance I cannot live without. Over the years, through consistent prayer and devoted study, God has progressively deepened my understanding of Scripture and has graciously used me as a life coach and instrument to help many people deepen their understanding of Scripture. In every facet of my purpose, I rely absolutely on Scripture to please God, for clear direction, for unerring guidance, for wisdom, and for understanding. Whenever I encounter uncertainty, I immediately know with unwavering confidence that I can seek sound wisdom within Scripture.

Let us ponder a hypothetical yet deeply revealing scenario: What would Jesus' life on earth have been like without God's verbal instruction? How would His ministry, assignments, destiny, and purpose have been affected if His life were absent from the adoption of Scripture and verbal information from God?

Consider what would have happened if Jesus had not received direct, verbal instruction from the Father. Think about the affirmation at His baptism: "This is My beloved Son, in whom I am well pleased." Imagine the absence of guidance through prayer or the agonizing clarity He experienced in Gethsemane. And what if Jesus had never read, studied, or internalized the Scriptures?

Without divine guidance, direct revelation, and the written Word, His identity and purpose would have crumbled. Who would He have claimed to be? What message would He have had to deliver? He would have been a man without a mandate, a prophet without prophecy, a king without a kingdom. His wisdom and authority, which astonished those who heard Him, would have been absent, for they stemmed directly from God.

How, then, would He have resisted Satan's cunning temptations in the wilderness? The biblical account is explicit: Jesus countered every trick of the devil with a direct quote from the book of Deuteronomy: "It is written…" Without the Scripture embedded in His heart and mind, providing an unshakeable bulwark of truth, His response could have differed. The critical moment when the Messiah triumphed over temptation, where humanity's hope was secured by obedience, would have been lost, leaving humankind in perpetual bondage.

What crowds would have followed Him, and with what anticipation, to learn about the kingdom of God? People flocked to Jesus not just for healing, but because He taught with an authority unlike any they had ever known. His words were life-giving, challenging, and revelatory. They spoke of a divine reality, a kingdom not of this world, yet available through salvation. The understanding of the kingdom, its laws, its grace, and its future was rooted in His perfect apprehension of God's eternal plan, revealed both directly and through the prophets. Without God's instruction, His teachings would have been mere human philosophy, lacking the power to transform hearts, to reveal ultimate truth, or to offer salvation. There would be no Sermon on the Mount, no parables illuminating heavenly mysteries, no new covenant articulated with divine precision. His ministry would have been an echo, not a seismic shift.

And how would He have led and prepared His chosen disciples, those whose obedience helped build the foundation of the Church, a part of God's redemptive plan? Jesus spent years teaching them, revealing the Father's heart, explaining the kingdom, and showing them how He was the fulfillment of all that was written in the Law and the Prophets.

He opened their minds to understand the Scriptures, connecting ancient prophecies to His life, death, burial, and resurrection. Without this grounding in Scripture, the disciples would have been left bewildered, without a clear commission, understanding of the Gospel, or the spiritual authority required to establish the nascent Church. Their mission would have been without purpose, their message without power. Their assignment without purpose. Their destiny without grace.

The reality, however, is a testament to His divine nature and perfect humanity. Jesus understood, exemplified, and demonstrated the paramount value of God's Word in fulfilling His purpose and assignments for the sake of His destiny. Every step of His earthly journey, every teaching, miracle, act of compassion, and ultimately, His sacrificial death and glorious resurrection, were in perfect alignment with the Father's instructions and the prophecies of the Old Testament.

Jesus lived the truth that "Man shall not live by bread alone, but on every word that comes from the mouth of God."

This truth serves as a powerful call to us today. It is my earnest hope that your love for God will be ignited and deepened, leading you with conviction to read, diligently study, believe with your whole heart, and walk daily in the transforming power of the Word of God.

Prayer Points and Scriptures to Pray

Revelatory Understanding and Acceptance of God's Word for You in Every Season of Your Life:
II Timothy 3:16-17 (NIV)—"All Scripture is God-breathed and is useful for teaching, rebuking, correcting, and training in righteousness, so that the servant of God may be thoroughly equipped for every good work."

Divine Guidance and Direction as You Read and Study the Word of God:
Psalms 119:105 (NIV)—"Your word is a lamp for my feet, a light on my path."

Holiness that is Not Defined by Societal Standards or Morals:
Leviticus 19:2 (NIV)—"Speak to the entire assembly of Israel and say to them: 'Be holy because I, the Lord your God, am holy.'"

Radical Obedience to God, Regardless of Your Feelings or Emotions:
Deuteronomy 10:12 (NIV)—"And now, Israel, what does the Lord your God ask of you but to fear the Lord your God, o walk in obedience to him, to love him, to serve the Lord your God with all your heart and with all your soul."

Continual Sanctification and Consecration unto the Lord:
2 Corinthians 7:1 (NIV)—"Therefore, since we have these promises, dear friends, let us purify ourselves from everything that
contaminates body and spirit, perfecting holiness out of reference
for God.

Affirmation to Declare Over Your Life
I believe and receive the Word of God as my lamp and light,
equipping me for every good work and guiding my steps with
wisdom and clarity (2 Tim. 3:16-17; Ps. 119:105). I stand firm
in faith, consecrated and set apart, confident that I am more
than a conqueror through Christ who strengthens and upholds
me, living boldly as a testimony of His grace, power, and faithfulness (2 Cor. 7:1; Isa. 41:10; Rom. 8:28, 37).

CHAPTER TWO

The Power of Prayer for Your Purpose

God commands us to "pray without ceasing" (1 Thess. 5:17). This is not a suggestion, but a directive, highlighting the crucial role prayer must play in the life of a believer. Neglecting prayer is a dangerous decision that can cause you to lack the necessary intimacy with God, leading you down a path of relentless destruction. If you fail to cultivate your relationship with God through consistent communication, you can become vulnerable to temptation, doubt, and ultimately, straying from His will.

Praying without ceasing is as vital as breathing. We do not think about every breath, yet our lungs continue to supply our bodies with oxygen. Breathing is natural. It is a function of life itself. Prayer ought to be similarly innate, an automatic aspect of our daily lives. Prayer fosters an open, constant line of communication with God, not just during formalized prayer times, but throughout every moment of the day. This means turning our thoughts, anxieties, joys, and concerns towards Him into a continuous stream of conversation, living in His presence, acknowledging His guidance, and seeking His wisdom in all that we do. By making prayer a habit, we cultivate a deeper relationship with God, allowing Him to shape and direct our lives according to His purpose.

Praying without ceasing requires self-discipline. Self-discipline in prayer is a cultivated virtue. It is a practice that demands intentionality, thrives on consistency, and is ultimately fueled by a willful desire for deep intimacy with God. Praying is a conscious choice to prioritize connection with God, carving out space and time amidst the demands of daily life. When these traits are intentionally established, a shift occurs: personal growth and spiritual maturity become innate, blossoming from the fertile ground of disciplined communion. This principle holds true—how you approach one thing often mirrors your approach to everything. Like a ripple effect, the discipline you cultivate in prayer spills over into other facets of your life. From my own experience, I have witnessed a tangible strengthening in various areas as I have become disciplined in prayer.

Self-discipline in prayer has afforded me the invaluable opportunity to gain insight into areas of my life that require adjustment, all for God's glory. He illuminated blind spots and redirected misguided paths. Through His loving direction, I have become more self-aware and attuned to my strengths and weaknesses. Prayer has yielded remarkable personal growth and a gradual elevation in my spiritual maturity. We are truly blessed to have unmerited favor and grace from God!

Having self-discipline in prayer cultivates a spirit of resilience, fostering steadfast consistency and nurturing mindfulness and perseverance in our daily lives. These qualities, in turn, produce tangible personal growth. They elevate us toward spiritual maturity and provide God's strength as we navigate the inevitable challenges of life. The comfort and strength derived from having an intimate relationship with God through prayer are unparalleled. It is a refuge, a source of support that transcends earthly limitations.

Self-discipline in prayer breeds resilience; we become stronger, more stable, and increasingly firm in faith. Stability empowers you to make sound decisions, aligning your choices with God's perfect will for your life. Being resilient in this way allows you to be mindful in your decision-making, grounding your choices in the unwavering guidance of God's will, absent from fleeting emotions or transient feelings. Ultimately, embracing self-discipline in prayer cultivates a richer, more robust character, one that reflects the very heart and mind of Christ.

Moses—A Man of God

When we consider Moses' life, I want you to understand the importance of prayer in relation to life's purpose and the value of maintaining a disciplined prayer life. Moses lived a life of prayer; it was an integral part of his life. His constant communication with God was not a ritual. It was a vital lifeline that guided his decisions, strengthened his resolve, and provided him with the wisdom necessary to lead the Hebrews out of slavery and towards the Promised Land. His intimate connection with God enabled him to navigate numerous challenges and overcome seemingly insurmountable obstacles. Prayer equipped him to hear God's instructions clearly, to receive His guidance in moments of uncertainty, and to intercede on behalf of his people. Ultimately, Moses' life highlights the power of consistent prayer as a catalyst for fulfilling one's divinely ordained purpose.

Exodus 19 stands as a monumental chapter in history. It showcases an unparalleled intersection of God's communication and human obedience, making it one of the most remarkable examples of prayer and purpose. It vividly illustrates the power of prayer as the conduit through which God's purpose is once again revealed and executed, setting the stage for the establishment of God's covenant with the Hebrews.

God outlined His immediate intentions to Moses during their dialogue. He reaffirmed His majestic leadership and steadfast commitment to guide the nascent nation through a journey already marked by the visible manifestation of His presence. The towering pillar of cloud by day and the illuminating pillar of fire by night were symbols of God's constant protection and direction towards the Promised Land.

In Exodus 19, God desired to personally address the entire Hebrew nation. Through Moses, He informed the people that He would descend upon Mount Sinai in a thick cloud, a palpable manifestation of His glory and power, from which He would speak to them directly. This was not a mere ethereal pronouncement. It came with meticulous and tangible instructions for preparation, including sanctification, setting strict boundaries around the mountain, and washing their clothes. God's directives were meant to prepare the people for an encounter with Him that was unimaginable. They would be introduced to the Holy One with reverence and awe.

The instructions also emphasized God's holiness and the seriousness of the covenant that was about to be made. Exodus 19 serves as the breathtaking prelude to one of many unforgettable moments in the Hebrew nation's foundation. The meticulous preparations, the awe-inspiring thunder and lightning, the trumpet blasts growing louder and louder, all orchestrated the stage for the revelation of the Ten Commandments in Exodus chapter 20. The Ten Commandments encompass both moral and spiritual principles, given in the secret place to Moses and presented to a prepared people. The key principle was prayer.

The life of Moses, particularly in these chapters, offers a compelling paradigm for us today. It powerfully demonstrates that prayer is not simply an auxiliary activity but the essential crucible in which divine purpose is forged and destiny is fulfilled. Moses' constant communion with God illustrates that living in your purpose is linked to consistent inquiry, fervent prayer, and receptive listening. Every major undertaking, every challenging situation, and every step toward the Promised Land, whether literal or spiritual, invariably demands specific direction and counsel from the Lord. Moses lived in close partnership with God. He sought the Lord with diligence and received clear direction, counsel, and strategic guidance.

For most of his leadership, Moses faithfully obeyed God. The singular, poignant instance of hitting the rock instead of speaking to it stands out precisely because it was an anomaly, a momentary lapse that starkly contrasted with his otherwise unblemished record of obedience and trust. This exception, in fact, only further underscores the critical importance of constant adherence to God's specific instructions, reinforcing that even the most seasoned leaders must remain vigilant in their obedience to God.

David—A Man After God's Heart

David, a strong man of God, is etched in the annals of faith as one who was "after God's own heart" (1 Sam. 3:14). This profound description speaks volumes about his character and relationship with God. But what does it truly mean to pursue God's heart? It is a journey intrinsically linked to a vibrant and consistent life of prayer. It is not possible to seek the heart of the Lord without a life of prayer. Prayer played a pivotal role in David's life, serving as the lifeline that connected him to the source of his strength and guidance. Psalm 23 is a powerful example of David's intimacy with God.

David's life was interwoven with hardship and triumph, divine favor and relentless persecution. When God removed His anointing from King Saul, a man who had strayed from God's path, and blessed David with mighty battle hands and strategic wisdom, the seeds of jealousy were sown in Saul's heart. Imagine the stark reality of spending years of your life in constant flight, tirelessly running and hiding from a King consumed by a murderous rage, a King who was supposed to hold a position of authority and respect. How would you cope with the constant murder threat looming over your head? How would you maintain hope in the face of such adversity? For David, God was his refuge, his hope in a seemingly hopeless situation.

The book of Psalms offers a deeply personal, unfiltered glimpse into the full spectrum of David's emotions. These poetic expressions unveil the highs of victory and the lows of despair, the moments of firm faith and times of crippling doubt, all experienced as he navigated the treacherous landscape of life while fleeing from the evil schemes of Saul's heart. Through Psalms, we witness David's raw vulnerability and steadfast commitment to seeking God's face amidst the storm.

Surely, the consistent discipline of praying without ceasing as God commands, cultivated a remarkable intimacy between David and God. Their intimacy fostered wisdom beyond his years, providing him with clarity and guidance from God in moments of uncertainty. It was through prayer that David discovered renewed hope, a restored heart, and the unshakeable assurance that he was not alone in his trials. His life stands as a testament to the transformative power of prayer, illustrating how consistent dialogue with God can sustain us through the darkest of times and lead us towards a life that mirrors His image.

From the examples of David and Moses, you can gain an important understanding of the value of a strong, unwavering, consistent, and deeply ingrained life of prayer. Their stories stand as testaments to the power that comes from continual communion with God. I encourage you to cultivate a life of prayer that transcends ritualistic patterns of praying in the morning, evening, and before meals. While those are valuable habits, I challenge you to delve deeper and develop a robust and vibrant life of prayer that surpasses the typical 10-to-15-minute supplications we often offer, relying on God as a lifeline in our daily lives. Yes, those brief moments are necessary, but they often fall short of establishing the deep connection necessary for sustained guidance and strength.

As you prepare to walk in your God-given purpose and face the enemy's inevitable attacks, remember that a strong, consistent prayer life is essential. It is an indispensable foundation for success, resilience, and faith. Prayer is an investment that yields dividends far beyond our imagination, providing wisdom, peace, and supernatural strength in both triumph and tribulation.

Prayer Points and Scriptures to Pray

Confidence, Faith, and Reassurance that God Hears Your Prayers:
I John 5:14-15 (NIV)—"This is the confidence we have in approaching God: that if we ask anything according to his will, he hears us. And if we know that he hears us, whatever we ask, we know that we have what we asked of him."

Grace to Live a Life of Prayer as You Pray in the Spirit and with Understanding:
Ephesians 6:18 (NIV)—"And pray in the Spirit on all occasions with all kinds of prayers and requests. With this in mind, be alert and always keep on praying for all the Lord's people."

Discipline in Prayer: A Grateful Pursuit of Deeper Intimacy with God
Colossians 4:2 (NIV)—"Devote yourselves to prayer, being watchful and thankful."

The Unquenchable Desire to Seek the Face and Mind of God:
Matthew 6:33 (NIV)—"But seek first his kingdom and his righteousness, and all these things will be given to you as well."

To be Clothed with Righteousness and Fervency to Pray Effectively:
James 5:16 (NIV)—"Therefore confess your sins to each other and pray for each other so that you may be healed. The prayer of a righteous person is powerful and effective."

Affirmation to Declare Over Your Life
I will approach God with confidence, devoting myself to prayer with gratitude and watchfulness, knowing that when I pray according to His will, He hears me and answers (1 John 5:14-15; Col. 4:2; Eph. 6:18). I will seek first His kingdom and righteousness, trusting that my prayers align me with His purpose, order my steps, and position me to walk boldly into the destiny He has prepared (Matt, 6:33; Jas. 5:16; Jer. 29:11; Psalm 37:23).

CHAPTER THREE

Foundational Tools to Find Your Purpose

I pray your desire to learn and live in your purpose does not supersede your desire to surrender and obey God. While striving to learn your purpose is commendable, it should never overshadow the primary goal of pleasing God through faith, surrender, and obedience. Living a purposeful life outside of God will lead to a life of accomplishment devoid of His glory. It will be a shameful outcome, in all honesty, literally spiritual death.

The analogy of a king in the Old Testament further illustrates this point. A king's role was multifaceted. It meant ruling justly, leading in battle, ensuring the safety and security of his people, and possessing the wisdom, knowledge, and understanding to govern effectively. King Saul, the first king of Israel, exemplified such. His anointment by God established kingship as his divinely ordained purpose. Scripture suggests that a person's purpose, like Saul's kingship, is illuminated by God's glory when actively integrating God's principles, morals, values, and way, which comes from full surrender and obedience.

According to the standards of Saul's time, his military victories, territorial expansion, establishment of a strong kingdom, and provision of national identity and security deemed him successful.

Saul's worldly successes, while impressive, may have been achieved at the cost of his obedience and surrender to God. Success in the eyes of the world does not necessarily equate to success in God's eyes. First Samuel 13-15 lays the groundwork for a further exploration of Saul's eventual downfall through disobedience, stressing the dangers of prioritizing worldly achievement over surrender and obedience. This highlights the importance of the initial warning against letting personal ambition overshadow surrender and obedience to God.

Obedience to God is one of the foundational principles essential for walking in your purpose. It is deeply intertwined with surrender, requiring full submission, consecration, and sanctification. When this level of surrender occurs, a profound shift takes place in a person's life. Intimacy with God begins to flourish, deepening to a point where He can entrust you with the revelation of your purpose.

Before that revelation comes, I encourage you to give your life to God, fully and completely, in every area, every facet, and every hidden corner. He desires all of you, not just parts. When you reach the place of total surrender, obedience becomes second nature. A heart rooted in surrender and obedience adds weight and value to your purpose.

Although surrender and obedience may not be strict prerequisites for receiving revelation of your purpose, I believe they position the heart of believers to carry the mantle of purpose and walk in it faithfully. Being firmly planted in these virtues is vital so that your life brings honor, not shame, to God's holy name.

Let me offer a simple analogy. Have you ever been to a restaurant and received poor service from a server? I have experienced wrong orders, inattentiveness, and disregard for basic etiquette. Why am I being served salmon when I asked for chicken? Who thought it was a good idea to bring me soda when I clearly ordered water? It is comical! I internally chuckle and hold no grudge or discontent.

I often think of myself as God's waiter, tasked with fulfilling His orders with radical obedience and surrender, not reluctance. While I sometimes wrestle with hesitation and ask clarifying questions, I keep this truth before me: obedience and surrender are reasonable, necessary, and required for intimacy and purpose. I encourage you to adopt the same posture as you seek revelation of your purpose.

As you continue to surrender and obey, begin operating in your spiritual gifts. Whether it is prophecy, encouragement, teaching, serving, giving, leadership, or mercy, these are gifts God has graciously given to His kingdom citizens. So, what is your gift? How are you using it? Is God receiving glory through your gift?

While you wait for your purpose to be revealed, ask Holy Spirit to guide you in fully activating your gift. Your gift was given for the sake of your purpose. To walk in purpose, you must also walk in your gifting. Ask Holy Spirit to help you sharpen and develop your gift so you can operate in excellence even while waiting.

Surrender. Obey. Utilize your gift. Follow the example of the Lord Jesus Christ. By living as He lived and doing what He said, I believe God will reveal your purpose in His perfect timing.

In the book of Ezekiel, God searched for a qualified prophetic candidate among the Hebrew priests and prophets. God found rebellious leaders whose hearts were turned away from Him. At 30 years old, Ezekiel was positioned as a priest. God ordained Ezekiel a prophet as he found Ezekiel surrendered, obedient, and positioned in his gifting. As you surrender, obey, and utilize your gift, I believe God will handpick you to walk boldly into your purpose, just like Ezekiel.

Now let's unpack additional foundational tools for revealing your purpose, found in the powerful message of Hebrews 11:6 and its implications, particularly as you seek God's purpose for your life. The scripture states, "But without faith it is impossible to please Him, for he who comes to God must believe that He is, and that He is a rewarder of those who diligently seek Him" (Heb. 11:6). This is not merely a nice sentiment. It is a foundational truth. It highlights the necessity of faith as the bedrock of our relationship with God. To approach Him, we must first acknowledge His existence and believe in Him as a rewarder, a God who actively and generously responds to those who earnestly seek Him.

Understanding this scripture should fuel your pursuit of the Lord for your divinely ordained purpose. He promises to reward those who diligently seek Him. But what does "diligence" truly entail? As defined by Webster's 1828 Dictionary, diligence is a "constant effort to accomplish what is undertaken." It is not a fleeting interest or a half-hearted attempt, but a persistent commitment to finding God.

The story of David, as illustrated in Psalm 34, provides a compelling example of this principle in action. Under immense pressure and fear for his life, David fled from Saul and found himself in the land of Gath, seeking refuge with the Philistine King, Abimelech. Ultimately, he sought refuge in a cave, a potentially dangerous place of vulnerability and uncertainty. It was in this desperate situation, while hidden away, that David penned Psalm 34 (KJV). In verse 4, he declares, "I sought the Lord, and He heard me, and delivered me from all my fears."

Consider the weight of those words. David was not seeking God from a position of comfort or strength, but from a place of genuine fear and the very real possibility of death. Yet, even in that dire circumstance, he sought the Lord, and God *heard* him. God *delivered* him. This emphasizes that our circumstances do not disqualify us from seeking God; in fact, they should drive us to pursue Him relentlessly.

The revelation here is that regardless of the challenges you face, regardless of how overwhelming your circumstances might seem, when you genuinely seek the Lord, He *will* answer you. The timing of that answer may vary. It may be five years down the road, a test of patience and faith, or it might be a near-instantaneous response. But the promise remains: God responds when we seek Him.

So, as you embark on this journey of seeking the Lord for your specific purpose, hold fast to this truth. Do not let doubt or discouragement creep in. Pray from a place of belief that He will answer. Believe that He *wants* to reveal His plan for your life. Believe that He *will* reward you as you diligently seek Him. Know that your "constant effort to accomplish what is undertaken" in seeking Him is not in vain. He sees your heart, He hears your prayers, and He will guide you to the purpose He has designed specifically for you. Rest assured that He will answer in His perfect timing, always right on time. Trust in His faithfulness, and continue to seek Him diligently, knowing that He is indeed a rewarder of those who do so.

I urge you to commit to memorizing Isaiah 40:31, "But those who wait on the Lord shall renew their strength; they shall mount up with wings like eagles, they shall run and not be weary, they shall walk and not faint." This is God's promise. As you patiently wait on the Lord, understand that He will infuse you with fresh strength, fortifying you against the current and future challenges. Weariness and weakness will lose their grip on your spirit as you lean on and into Him. Waiting on the Lord is an active posture of trust, faith, and expectation.

I am a living testament to the power of waiting on the Lord and the renewal it brings. Several years ago, I earnestly sought God for something vital to the command He had given me. While waiting, unexpected individuals offered guidance and support, propelling me closer to obtaining what I needed. It took a year to materialize, but looking back, I realize that God was meticulously fortifying me during that waiting period. He was preparing me not only to receive what I asked for but also to sustain it and utilize it effectively.

Now that you grasp the value of waiting on the Lord, let's delve into the importance of believing that you will receive when you ask. Mark 11:24 says, "Therefore I say to you, whatever things you ask when you pray, believe that you receive them, and you will have them." It is a nice sentiment and a principle of God.

So, ask yourself: Do I genuinely believe that God will answer my prayers? Do I sincerely believe that He will respond to my request to reveal my purpose and the assignments He has in store for me? If there is a seed of doubt, I encourage you to spend more time in prayer, asking God to search your heart and remove any hesitancy or unbelief that may be hindering you. Unbelief can cloud your perception and prevent you from fully embracing God's promises.

The story of the father whose son was afflicted with a deaf and mute demon serves as a powerful reminder that God can cure our unbelief. The father, aware of his son's affliction, initially brought him to Jesus' disciples for deliverance, but they were unable to help. Desperate, he then brought his son to Jesus. Jesus inquired, "How long has this been happening to him?" The father replied, "From childhood. And often he has thrown him both into the fire and into the water to destroy him. But if You can do anything, have compassion on us and help us." Jesus responded, "If you can believe, all things are possible to him who believes. Immediately, the father of the child cried out and said with tears, "Lord, I believe; help my unbelief!" (Mark 9:24).

Notice that the father, despite his faith in Jesus' ability to heal, still harbored a degree of unbelief. Can you relate to this father? Do you sometimes pray with doubts lingering in your heart? Have past experiences or challenging circumstances eroded your faith? It is a human struggle, but it does not have to define you.

If you find yourself struggling with unbelief, I implore you to follow the father's example and ask God to help your unbelief. Cultivate a practice of journaling answered prayers and moments when you have witnessed God's intervention. Regularly revisit your journal to rekindle your faith, remember God's faithfulness, and reinforce the truth that He stands by His promises. First John 5:14-15 offers further reassurance, "Now this is the confidence that we have in Him, that if we ask anything according to His will, He hears us. And if we know that He hears us, whatever we ask, we know that we have the petitions that we have asked of Him."

Focus on this: God desires you to fulfill the purpose He has for your life. He wants you to obtain everything in your destiny. Therefore, it aligns perfectly with His will for you to be aware of that purpose and in alignment with destiny. As you pray with a heart brimming with belief, you can be confident that He hears you and will respond. What a magnificent and attentive God we serve!

Now that you understand the value of diligently seeking God, the importance of waiting on Him, and the power of a believing heart, stand confident that He hears you and will answer. Open your heart to receive your purpose, destiny, and assignments. Be ready for whatever else God desires to speak into your life. If you are finding it difficult to open your heart, sincerely ask God to prepare it for what He wants to reveal.

Once your heart is prepared, ask God to reveal your purpose, destiny, and assignments. Take a notebook and pen, find a quiet place, and remain in His presence until He responds. Listen attentively, not just for a booming voice but also for a gentle whisper, a prompting, or a sense of clarity.

It may seem too simple, but I have successfully coached many people with this process. Do not overcomplicate the process. Continuously repeat these steps until you receive your purpose from the Lord. I cannot say it enough; God answers prayer, and He will reveal His plan for your life when you seek Him with a sincere and believing heart. Dare to persist until you receive that revelation.

Prayer Points and Scriptures to Pray

Repentance for Impatience While Waiting on the Lord:
Proverbs 14:29 (NIV)—"Whoever is patient has great understanding, but one who is quick-tempered displays folly."

Grace to Wait on the Lord:
Psalm 27:14 (NIV)—"Wait for the Lord; be strong and take heart and wait for the Lord."

Trust in God's Timing:
Isaiah 60:22 (NIV)—"The least of you will become a thousand, the smallest a mighty nation. I am the Lord; In its time, I will do this swiftly."

Patience to Sit and Commune with God:
Psalm 37:7 (NIV)—"Be still before the Lord and wait patiently for him; do not fret when people succeed in their ways, when they carry out their wicked schemes."

Developing a Deeper Relationship God Can Trust
Jeremiah 29:13 (NIV)—"You will seek me and find me when you seek me with all your heart."

Affirmation to Declare Over Your Life
I repent of impatience and surrender my timeline to the Lord, choosing to walk in His peace and wait with strength and courage, knowing that patience brings wisdom and that waiting refines my faith (Prov. 14:29; Ps. 27:14; Isa. 60:22). I quiet my soul before Him, seeking the Lord with all my heart and anchoring my hope in His promises, confident that in His perfect timing He will order my steps and fulfill His plans for my life (Ps. 37:7; Jer. 29:13; Psalm 37:23).

CHAPTER FOUR

My Journey to My Purpose

As a child, a heavy question weighed on my heart. What was the intentionality of my life? I wrestled with the idea that if God truly desired my life to have purpose, why wasn't I made aware of it? Why was I brought into existence when there seemed to be so many others who were "better" than me? What unique value could I possibly add to the earth? These questions swirled within me, forming a cloud of confusion and doubt that shadowed my early years.

Growing up as the middle child in a family of six—with four boisterous boys and two girls, and me as the eldest daughter— only amplified these feelings. I reasoned that surely there could not be anything God needed *me* to do that my more capable siblings could not accomplish. This thought fueled a growing sense of inadequacy, a feeling that I was somehow less worthy, less deserving of a divine purpose.

This internal struggle fostered a deep-seated battle with low self-esteem, worth, and confidence. My challenges were compounded by the fact that I was often the only black girl in many of my elementary school classes. This exposed me to the harsh realities of racism and discrimination, experiences that left deep emotional scars and contributed to a plethora of internal issues. I could not comprehend why I was devalued and disrespected simply because of the color of my skin. I was a quiet child, always polite and respectful to my peers and teachers. I genuinely gave no one a reason to be cruel towards me, yet the prejudice persisted, leaving me feeling confused and broken.

Having such low self-esteem and a profound lack of self-worth created an internal barrier to accepting God's love. It was a paradox I could not reconcile. How could He possibly love someone like me—the "ugly black girl with nappy hair," as I perceived myself through the distorted lens of societal biases? The concept seemed utterly impossible, a distant dream reserved for others, not for someone as flawed and unworthy as I felt I was.

Throughout this tumultuous period, I kept my internal battles hidden, never discussing my struggles with anyone. Yet, God knew. He saw the pain in my heart, the silent tears I shed, and the longing for meaning that consumed me. One day, as I lay in bed, overwhelmed with despair and even desiring my end at the tender age of seven, God spoke to me. His words were simple, yet profound enough to alter the very trajectory of my life. In a still, soft voice, yet with undeniable strength and unwavering confidence, God said, "I love you." This simple declaration, filled with divine reassurance, gave me more hope than any words of comfort from my parents, siblings, friends, or even my church family could have. It was a personal revelation, a direct connection to the source of all love and worth.

At the age of seven, shortly after this profound experience, God called me to the ministry. I was outside, simply minding my own business, when I heard His voice, loud and clear. To say I was reluctant would be an understatement. I certainly was not willing to be a 'preacher,' but I was undeniably willing to serve the Lord. My love for God was genuine and unwavering. This love compelled me to obey His command and be baptized at eight years old. I fully immersed myself in faith, being baptized in Jesus' name and receiving the precious gift of the Holy Ghost, endued with power, and my heavenly language, at the age of nine.

Happiness filled my soul, as I believed from a young age that my purpose in life was crystal clear: to preach the Gospel. In my youthful naiveté, I thought all I needed to do was live a holy and righteous life, preach the Gospel, and life would be peachy keen. I was so wrong! In fact, I lived with this simplified idea for over 20 years, completely unaware of its flaws and incompleteness.

At seventeen, I diligently completed the necessary requirements and became a licensed minister through the Pentecostal Assemblies of the World. I began preaching all over the state, sharing my testimony and spreading the word of God. Yet even amid God's presence in my life and apparent ministry success, I still felt a persistent longing for something deeper. I felt like I was missing a crucial piece of the puzzle, but I could not quite identify what it was. How could I possibly be missing something when, in my mind, I was operating at my prime?

At twenty-two, I was in my junior year of college, ambitiously double-majoring in sociology and social work. I was also heavily involved at my local church home, relentlessly serving the Lord in various capacities. During this busy season of my life, I met a young man who was experiencing significant turmoil in his life. I prayed with him, offered words of encouragement, and collected his contact information to continue praying for him. About a week later, I contacted him, and we scheduled a meeting in person so that I could further minister to him. As fate would have it, or more truthfully, as the consequence of my actions, I discovered a few weeks later that I was pregnant.

This was not how I envisioned my life unfolding. The reality of being a pregnant minister, who was boldly preaching against fornication and living a life of celibacy and purity, was a stark contrast to the image I had carefully cultivated. The thought of entering my senior year of college, without the financial resources or emotional stability to raise a child, filled me with dread.

How could I have allowed this to happen? Who would care for this child while I juggled the demanding requirements of my bachelor's degree? How could I possibly attend college while pregnant? What would everyone think of me? These thoughts relentlessly penetrated and haunted my mind, leading to countless depressing and tearful days and nights. I could not grasp how one decision, one impulsive act, could change the entire course of my life so drastically. How could I have been so stupid and naïve?

My child's father and I decided to pursue a relationship for the sake of our unborn child. After several months of navigating the complexities of our situation, we became engaged and began to formulate a plan for a successful life and marriage. However, as is often the case with plans made under duress, everything spiraled out of control, and our relationship abruptly ceased.

Throughout my pregnancy, despite the shame and confusion, I never stopped praying. I clung to the memory of God's words to me at the age of seven, "I love you," and found solace in that unwavering truth. Yet, once again, I struggled to fully accept His love. How could He possibly love someone like me, who once lived in sin, after previously preaching so vehemently against it? The hypocrisy gnawed at my conscience, making it difficult to believe that I was worthy of His grace.

When my son was born, a new sense of purpose began to emerge. I realized that my immediate purpose was to be a mother, to nurture and care for this precious life entrusted to me. I also felt a stirring to share my testimony of redemption with the world. Throughout my challenging pregnancy, several people at church, aware of my situation, consistently shared with me that my story would ultimately help someone else.

I was sold on the idea, but I was not quite ready to publicly share the raw truth. I needed time to heal, to process the trauma I had caused by engaging in sin, and to find a way to articulate my experience with honesty and vulnerability. For the rest of my life, I was determined to remain single and travel the world with my son, sharing my powerful testimony of how I strayed away from God and how He, in His infinite mercy, redeemed my soul. Again, I was wrong. This was not my ultimate purpose.

When my son was three months old, I went to a local diner and met a friendly, yet shy, man of God. He shared with me that he had recently moved to Washington State. He was taking a break from his demanding work life, spending his days immersed in prayer and reading the Bible. We talked for over three hours that day, and it was evident that he possessed a genuine love for the Lord. We became friends, even though I was extremely hesitant to befriend any man again after my previous relationship.

This time, however, the dynamic was different. He was ministering to me during a time when my life was in turmoil. He listened without judgment, offered wise counsel, and provided unwavering support. Through his gentle guidance, I repented of my sins and fully surrendered my life back to God. I truly believe that God sent this young man into my life to minister to me, intercede on my behalf, and exemplify God's unconditional love.

Several months later, Jeffrey and I began "courting," an old-school term that essentially means dating with intentionality and purpose. We took a vow of celibacy and committed to honoring God in our relationship. After four years of intentional courting, we were married. My life purpose shifted again, to preach the Gospel, be a devoted wife, and raise our son while ministering to folks within my sphere of influence. Yet again, I was so wrong!

A year and a half into our marriage, God instructed me to leave my home church, the very church where I grew up, the church that was a constant in my life since childhood. Having recently given birth to my second child, I had not received any instructions as to which church to attend next. I was perplexed, but I trusted God's plan, even if I could not see it at the time.

God began to systematically strip me of the religious mindset that captivated my heart and stunted my spiritual growth. I was not aware of how deeply ingrained my religious beliefs were, because I genuinely believed I possessed a strong, authentic relationship with the Lord. This season of my life was incredibly painful because I suddenly found myself without a church home and I felt abandoned by God in the desert.

While in this metaphorical desert, God ministered to me and revealed my true purpose. When I stepped into who I was created to be—my purpose—I realized prayer, scripture, intimacy with God, fasting, obedience, surrender, and utilizing my gifts were the primary keys that unlocked the door. I came to the profound understanding that my purpose is not intrinsically linked to a specific church building, the identity of the person I am married to, or even the well-being of my children. The timing of this revelation was perfect, aligning with the season of stripping and refining that God was orchestrating in my life.

You may have experienced seasons in your life where you felt like God abandoned you and your life was utterly meaningless. Please be reassured that "all things work together for good to them that love God, to them who are called according to his purpose" (Romans 8:28 KJV). Be encouraged by my testimony, knowing that God has not abandoned you, even when it feels like He has. He is true to His Word, which says He will never leave you nor forsake you (Hebrews 13:5).

I admonish you to never leave Him, like I did, but remain faithful, trusting that He is working behind the scenes, even when you cannot see it. Find rest and peace knowing that He created you intentionally, with a unique purpose that will ultimately impact the earth in ways you may not even comprehend. Your value is inherent, your purpose is divinely ordained, and His love for you is unwavering and eternal.

Prayer Points and Scriptures to Pray

Embrace Who God Fearfully and Wonderfully Made You to Be
Psalm 139:14 (NIV)—"I praise you because I am fearfully and wonderfully made; your works are wonderful. I know that full well."

A Pledge to Worship God with Your Life:
John 4:24 (NIV)—"God is spirit, and his worshipers must worship in the Spirit and in truth."

Celebrate God's Handiwork and Your Identity as His Masterpiece
Ephesians 2:10 (NIV)—"For we are God's handiwork, created in Christ Jesus to do good works, which God prepared in advance for us to do."

Appreciation and Acceptance of God's Love:
Psalm 63:3 (NIV)—"Because your love is better than life, my lips will glorify you."

Continual Surrender Fully to God's Sovereign Design and Calling
Isaiah 43:1 (NIV)—"But now, this is what the Lord says—he who created you, Jacob, he who formed you, Israel: 'Do not fear, for I have redeemed you; I have summoned you by name; you are mine.'"

Affirmation to Declare Over Your Life
I praise God for I am fearfully and wonderfully made, His handiwork created in Christ Jesus to do good works, and I worship Him in Spirit and in truth, glorifying Him with my life (Ps. 139:14; Eph. 2:10; John 4:24). Because His love is better than life, I embrace my identity as His masterpiece, living in gratitude and surrender as I walk in the fullness of His purpose (Ps. 63:3).

CHAPTER FIVE

Effective Fasting in Your Purpose

B efore fasting, it is of paramount importance to approach it with wisdom and discernment. I strongly urge you to seek guidance from God through prayer, asking Him for clarity and confirmation regarding this discipline. Simultaneously, it is crucial to consult your physician to ensure that fasting is medically safe for you, considering your individual health status and any potential risks. **Do not initiate a fast until you have received clear permission from God and a medical clearance from your doctor.** Your well-being, both spiritual and physical, should be your utmost priority.

I encourage you to take a moment to reflect on your own experiences with fasting. What challenges have you experienced when you fast? Do you believe you fast effectively with proven results? Does God speak to you during your fasts, offering guidance and direction? These are important questions to ask ourselves as we seek growth in our relationship with God and alignment with the purpose God has for our lives.

Effective fasting, when undertaken with the right intention and understanding, unlocks extraordinary divine power within you and propel you to a deeper, more intimate relationship with God. It is not merely abstaining from food; it is about intentionally expecting to hear from God. It is crucial to understand that simply skipping meals for an extended period does not constitute a true fast. In fact, you can fast for 72 hours and still not see any results.

True fasting requires quieting the distractions and noise of daily life. It means intentionally abstaining from food or water, depending on the type of fast. During this time, you devote yourself to prayer, spend time in God's Word, and engage in worship, thanksgiving, praise, and communion with Him. This is the effective formula that guides a meaningful and impactful fast. If you do not follow it sincerely, you may merely experience hunger and missed meals without truly tapping into the phenomenal spiritual benefits of fasting.

Fasting can be understood as a symbolic act of dying to the flesh, our sinful nature. As we abstain from physical nourishment, we naturally become more spiritually alert, positioning our souls to be transformed by God. It is a deliberate choice to prioritize our spiritual hunger over our physical desires.

Personally, during times of fasting, I have experienced a heightened sense of spiritual awareness both during and after the fast. My ability to hear from God becomes clearer, and I feel closer to Him. It is a time of profound intimacy and spiritual growth that I value more than the consumption of food.

Let's delve deeper into the subject of food, tracing its significance from the beginning of human existence. When God created man and placed him in the Garden of Eden, humanity was physically sustained by the pure and unadulterated bounty of the earth. Food was a gift, a direct provision from God. However, after Adam and Eve disobeyed God's command and partook of the forbidden fruit, the idyllic conditions were irrevocably altered. Because of their sin, God declared an increase in the pain of childbirth for the woman and cursed the ground for man's sake, decreeing that it would henceforth produce thorns and thistles.

It is a point of considerable reflection that God, in His warning, stated that upon eating from the tree of knowledge of good and evil, they would "surely die." Yet, in a literal sense, Adam and Eve did not immediately cease to exist physically. Their initial disobedience resulted in a spiritual death, a separation from God's presence. God, in His holiness, cannot abide in the presence of sin. This separation marked a fundamental shift in the relationship between God and mankind.

Spiritual separation impacted our very being, changing our natural appetite. Genesis 3:17-19 KJV poignantly describes this alteration: "And unto Adam he said, Because thou hast hearkened unto the voice of thy wife, and hast eaten of the tree, of which I commanded thee, saying, Thou shalt not eat of it: cursed is the ground for thy sake; in sorrow shalt thou eat of it all the days of thy life; Thorns also and thistles shall it bring forth to thee; and thou shalt eat the herb of the field; In the sweat of thy face shalt thou eat bread, till thou return unto the ground; for out of it wast thou taken: for dust thou art, and unto dust shalt thou return."

The shift in our appetite, born from the curse upon the ground, occurs in the gradual deterioration and eventual demise of our physical bodies. In essence, the food we consume is cursed, as is the ground and its producer. The consumption of this "cursed food" inherently leads to illness and disease, as it gradually takes a toll on our mortal bodies. Beyond food itself, the act of working to obtain sustenance and the effort required to cultivate and procure it further contribute to the wear and tear on our bodies, ultimately affecting our mortality. Consider the implications of rejecting "cursed food" for the sake of life. Consider how consciously choosing to abstain from things that contribute to our physical decline and to prioritize time with God through fasting can draw God's attention. Once again, when you fast, your spirit must cleave to God for survival in the absence of that which is cursed.

In this season of your life, as you pursue God's divine plan, consider the potential of fasting. Fasting can act as a powerful tool that allows God to strip away all unrighteousness, all that is unholy, all sin, transgression, doubt, reluctance, fear, shame, and iniquity that may be within you. This process of purification positions you to represent Him appropriately, without bringing shame to His Holy name. Fasting, therefore, becomes a pathway to spiritual cleansing and alignment with God's purpose.

Please understand that your God-given purpose requires the discipline of fasting. Stepping into your purpose without the preparation and spiritual empowerment that fasting provides can be dangerous and ultimately unfruitful. You need the many benefits of fasting to remain spiritually alert, gain crucial insight and instruction from God, and mature in your faith. Fasting is a vital tool for navigating your path and destiny.

Throughout both the Old and New Testaments, we witness fasting as a necessary practice for God's people to elevate in Him. While fasting should not be viewed as the only or ultimate spiritual practice, it is undoubtedly a powerful tool for receiving revelation. As you navigate the complexities of life and seek to live out your purpose, divine revelation is essential for guiding your steps and decisions from your assignments to your destiny.

While fasting, I often reflect on its significance in the story of Esther. During the Persian reign under King Ahasuerus, Haman was elevated to the second-highest position of power in the kingdom.

Haman was not a Persian royal or noble. He was an Agagite, a descendant of the ancient Canaanites. Although a minor detail, such carries immense historical weight, for it signifies a lineage steeped in ancient enmity, harkening back to the conflict between the Israelites and the Amalekites, whose king, Agag, was famously spared by Saul before being executed by Samuel (1 Sam. 15). This background subtly hints at a deep-seated, almost primordial hatred that Haman may have harbored for the Israelites.

To solidify Haman's elevated status and demand for universal respect, a royal decree commanded that all government officials and citizens prostrate themselves and bow in obeisance whenever Haman passed. Day after day, as Haman traversed the palace grounds, basking in the forced reverence of the court, Mordecai, the Israelite who sat at the king's gate, watched. He alone remained standing, refusing to bend a knee or bow his head. His defiance was not a matter of disrespect for the king, but rather a deeper conviction. His faith in God would not permit him to bestow such honor on a mortal.

Initially, Haman might have dismissed it as an oversight, but as the blatant insubordination persisted, his pride, already inflated, began to fester. When curious or perhaps malicious servants inquired about Mordecai's peculiar behavior, they eventually revealed his ethnic identity: he was an Israelite. Haman's fury, once focused on a single man, metastasized into an all-consuming hatred for an entire people. It was not enough to punish Mordecai; the root cause, his Israeli DNA, must be eradicated. With cunning words and likely exaggerated tales of Israeli insubordination or disloyalty, Haman successfully poisoned the king's ear, persuading Ahasuerus to enact a horrifying decree: the complete annihilation of all Israelites throughout the vast Persian Empire.

In a twist of fate, the date for this monstrous act was decided not by strategic planning or reasoned judgment, but by sheer chance. Haman, in his superstitious arrogance, consulted the 'pur,' the ancient, sacred lots or dice, believing he was consulting the heavens. But he was unknowingly setting the stage for God's intervention. Haman cast the lots, and the grim harvest date was set: the thirteenth day of the twelfth month, Adar, approximately eleven months away.

On this designated day, every Israeli man, woman, and child, regardless of age or status, was to be legally slaughtered, and their property plundered. Following this decree of mass murder, the scene shifts to a chilling display of indifference and ghoulish celebration. Haman, buoyed by his perceived triumph, and King Ahasuerus, oblivious or indifferent to the enormity of what he had sanctioned, raised their goblets in a celebratory feast within the opulent palace. While throughout the provinces, Israeli communities were plunged into despair and mourning, the architects of their doom toasted their success, reveling in their power and the impending destruction.

When faced with the horrifying news of a genocidal decree against her people, Queen Esther bravely called for a desperate and communal fast among all the Israelites in Susa. This was no ordinary fast; it was an act of humility and an urgent plea to God, a three-day fast from food and water in which Esther herself pledged to participate alongside her people. Her desperate hope was to gain favor to approach King Ahasuerus, her husband, an act punishable by death if she were not summoned. Her mission was perilous: to expose and dismantle Haman's insidious, evil plan to annihilate every Israelite within the Persian Empire.

The results of the fervent, nationwide fast were undeniably clear and divinely orchestrated. God moved powerfully, granting Esther extraordinary favor, courage, and strategic wisdom. When she approached the throne unbidden, the king, against all protocol, miraculously extended his golden scepter, sparing her life and opening the door for her plea. Esther, exercising remarkable discernment, hosted not one, but two banquets, masterfully building suspense and lulling Haman into a false sense of security and elevated pride. It was during the second climactic banquet that Esther courageously unveiled Haman's genocidal intent, exposing him not only as an enemy of her people but also as a direct threat to the queen herself. The dramatic revelation led to Haman's swift and just destruction, as he was impaled on the very gallows he had prepared for Mordecai, Esther's cousin. Ultimately, through divine intervention, the Israelites were miraculously spared, and their would-be oppressor was defeated.

The enduring courage of Esther serves as a potent and consistent reminder to me that genuine, effective fasting, coupled with earnest prayer and a posture of humility and dependence, captures God's attention. It is a spiritual discipline that can dramatically shift insurmountable circumstances, paving the way for God's intervention not only for us but also for the critical needs of others, demonstrating God's sovereign power in the face of human impossibility.

Consider the powerful testimony of Moses. He fasted for forty days while communing with God on Mount Sinai. During this time, he received the Ten Commandments, a powerful document written by the finger of God. The Ten Commandments were not merely a list of rules to maintain societal order; they represented the foundational stage of the Hebrews' development into a nation destined to inhabit the Promised Land, becoming a people and a place where God could dwell. The starting point for this transformation was Moses' consecrated life before the Lord, fueled by prayer, fasting, and faithful obedience to God's commands.

Does this resonate with your journey? Like Moses, we are called to dedicate our lives to God. He is drawn to prayer, fasting, and obedience to His commands. When we pursue these disciplines, we open ourselves to His guidance, direction, power, and presence.

Fasting serves a multitude of spiritual purposes, as a powerful spiritual discipline for those seeking a deeper walk with God. It is a consecrated act through which we can wholeheartedly submit ourselves and humbly prostrate before God, acknowledging His supreme sovereignty. Fasting also provides a focused avenue to seek God's will with intention, gain clarity on His purposes, and align our lives with His. Furthermore, it is a potent tool for sincere repentance and spiritual cleansing. Fasting purifies our hearts and draws us into God's holiness. Many also fast to intercede selflessly for others, bearing their burdens before God's throne. It is a crucial step of preparation for a significant divine mission, readying oneself for God's specific assignment.

A powerful illustration of these principles is found in Acts 13:2-3, depicting a pivotal moment in the early Church:

As they ministered to the Lord and fasted, the Holy Spirit said, "Now separate to Me Barnabas and Saul for the work to which I have called them." Then, having fasted and prayed, and laid hands on them, they sent them away (Acts 13:2-3).

Here, we witness a compelling truth: it was *during* a consecrated fast and worship that clear, godly guidance was provided. Specifically, Barnabas and Saul received a direct and specific assignment from the Holy Ghost. The response from the community was phenomenal: initiating a unified, immediate communal fast, accompanied by fervent prayer and impartation through the laying on of hands. This focused preparation yielded fruitful results in the kingdom. The Holy Ghost evidently was with Barnabas and Saul as they journeyed, preaching and teaching about Yeshua and converting many souls to Christ. Their ministry became a testament to the power unleashed through fasting, prayer, and worship.

Please understand that the discipline of fasting often transcends individual needs or personal desires. While it can certainly bring personal breakthroughs, its ultimate scope is far greater. When you fast with your soul and spirit focused on God's purpose, the blessings that follow are not merely for personal benefit. They also bring divine preparation, clear guidance, and steady direction. These come directly from God to advance His eternal kingdom and empower you to fulfill your unique assignment on the earth.

Indeed, fasting is infinitely grander than the temporal discomfort of hunger pains. Consider the monumental impact Paul (formerly Saul) and Barnabas had on the early Christian movement. Their full submission to God, cemented through consistent fasting, fervent prayer, and worship, laid foundational stones for the global spread of the Gospel. Take a moment to reflect on the incredible transformation God could bring through your life. Imagine what He might do if you fully surrendered to Him with that same devotion. Embrace fasting as a spiritual discipline. Commit to continual, fervent prayer. Pour out your heart in worship to Him every day. The potential for God's presence and power exemplified in the earth through you is immeasurable.

Prayer Points and Scriptures to Pray

Spirit-Led Direction for Fasting:

John 14:26 (NIV)—"But the Advocate, the Holy Spirit, whom the Father will send in my name, will teach you all things and will remind you of everything I have said to you."

Understanding Effective Fasting and Its Spiritual Impact:

Isaiah 58:2-3 (NIV)—"For day after day they seek me out; they seem eager to know my ways, as if they were a nation that does what is right and has not forsaken the commands of its God. They ask me for just decisions and seem eager for God to come near them. 'Why have we fasted,' they say, 'and you have not seen it? Why have we humbled ourselves, and you have not noticed?' Yet on the day of your fasting, you do as you please and exploit all your workers. Your fasting ends in quarreling and strife, and in striking each other with wicked fists. You cannot fast as you do today and expect your voice to be heard on high. Is this the kind of fast I have chosen, only a day for people to humble themselves? Is it only for bowing one's head like a reed and for lying in sackcloth and ashes? Is that what you call a fast, a day acceptable to the Lord? Is not this the kind of fasting I have chosen, to loose the chains of injustice and untie the cords of the yoke, to set the oppressed free and break every yoke? Is it not to share your food with the hungry and to provide the poor wanderer with shelter; when you see the naked, to clothe them, and not to turn away from your own flesh and blood?"

Joyful Heart Posture While Fasting:

Zechariah 8:19 (NIV)—"This is what the Lord Almighty says: 'The fasts of the fourth, fifth, seventh and tenth months will become joyful and glad occasions and happy festivals for Judah. Therefore love truth and peace.'"

Humility to Fast in Secret:
Matthew 6:16-18 (NIV)— "When you fast, do not look somber as the hypocrites do, for they disfigure their faces to show others they are fasting. Truly I tell you, they have received their reward in full. But when you fast, put oil on your head and wash your face, so that it will not be obvious to others that you are fasting, but only to your Father, who is unseen; and your Father, who sees what is done in secret, will reward you.

Humility Before the Lord During Your Fast So He Will Hear You:
Ezra 8:21-23 (NIV)— "There, by the Ahava Canal, I proclaimed a fast, so that we might humble ourselves before our God and ask him for a safe journey for us and our children, with all our possessions. I was ashamed to ask the king for soldiers and horsemen to protect us from enemies on the road, because we told the king, the gracious hand of our God is on everyone who looks to him, but his great anger is against all who forsake him. So we fasted and petitioned our God about his, and he answered our prayer."

Affirmation to Declare Over Your Life
As I fast, I walk in the Spirit who teaches me and answers when I call (John 14:26; Ezra 8:21-23; Matt. 6:16-18). My fasting is a holy offering that breaks chains, strengthens my spirit, and aligns me with God's purpose, positioning me for breakthrough and destiny in His perfect will (Isa. 58; Zechariah 8:19).

CHAPTER SIX

Cultivation in Your Purpose

Isn't it an exhilarating moment when God reveals the very essence of your existence, your purpose? It is like finding the missing piece of a puzzle you have been unknowingly assembling your whole life; the compass needle finally points true after years of wandering aimlessly.

I can honestly say that when God revealed my purpose, it was not just exciting; it was an electric surge of unbridled joy, a sense of "Aha!" that resonated through every fiber of my being. I was extremely ecstatic, enveloped with jubilation that made the world seem to snap into sharp focus. In that instant, I felt ready to roll my sleeves up, to dive headfirst into putting my hands to the plow, to hit the ground running with an irrepressible drive.

There was a rush of adrenaline, a sense of invincibility that convinced me there was nothing and no one that could stop me from fulfilling my purpose. I felt like an unstoppable force, bulletproof, if that is possible. However, with the wisdom of hindsight and a deeper understanding of God's principles, I caution against this immediate, headlong rush. That initial, powerful surge of enthusiasm, while a beautiful gift, can also be blinding.

When revelation occurs, whether it manifests as a dream, a vision, an undeniable sense in the spirit, or even the clear, unmistakable voice of God, the work is far from over. Regardless of the delivery method God uses, the next steps are clear and non-negotiable: write, pray, and cultivate. In that exact order. We often harbor this prevalent yet flawed misconception that, by some process of osmosis, God will provide, and we can go forth in faith and operate flawlessly in our purpose.

This is a dangerous presumption; spiritual laziness dressed as faith. While I wholeheartedly believe that the Holy Spirit does indeed download excellence, bestowing His blueprint, equipping us with inherent gifts, and supplying divine wisdom, the truth is that you must cultivate what He has given you.

First, write: As soon as the revelation strikes, capture it. Every detail, every impression, every word. Write it down to prevent memory distortion or fading over time.

Second, pray: Once documented, take it to God. Engage in a sustained, active dialogue with the Holy Spirit about what He has shown you. Seek deeper understanding, discernment, and wisdom for its implementation. Pray for clarity, for confirmation, for the sanctification of the purpose itself. This is where you move from passive reception to active partnership with Holy Spirit.

Third, cultivate: This is the phase of nurturing, developing, and preparing the ground. A precious seed of purpose, no matter how divinely planted, requires careful tending. This means studying, learning, growing, practicing, developing skills, and preparing your internal and external environment for its manifestation. It is not just about waiting; it is about actively stewarding the gift, honing the raw talent, and tilling the fertile field of your life.

Fourth: Repeat steps one through three for the rest of your life. As you grow into the fullness of who God created you to be, it is essential that you keep writing, praying, and cultivating. At every new level, you must invite the Holy Spirit to teach you once again how to pray, study Scripture, walk in obedience, use your giftings, submit to God, and cultivate faithfully. This rhythm ensures ongoing growth and maturity in God.

Even the most magnificent divine revelation can lie dormant, become misdirected, or wither due to lack of nurturing. Purpose and assignments are a partnership with Holy Spirit, a sacred trust that demands our active and thoughtful participation. That initial ecstasy is a powerful ignition, but the journey requires diligent, prayerful cultivation. Prayer is necessary because it is the place where you can find solutions to execute God's plan for your life.

For example, if someone's purpose is to establish a school that offers children a quality Christian education, my conviction is unwavering: God will indeed provide the requisite resources. This is not only about financial capital; it encompasses the provision of the right individuals, strategic opportunities, timely wisdom, and the very means to actualize that vision. However, this provision is not an invitation to passivity or a justification for negligence. It posits a partnership, a covenant, where our faith is met with our earnest endeavor. True spiritual maturity demands that we diligently pursue and acquire the essential knowledge and practical wisdom indispensable for the successful launch and sustainable operation of such a monumental undertaking.

Consider the multifaceted landscape of requirements. You will need a deep understanding of local zoning laws, educational ordinances, and accreditation standards. Operational expertise is

paramount, encompassing curriculum development, effective ped-
agogical strategies, sound financial management, and well-struc-
tured administrative systems. Staffing is more than hiring. It
involves recruitment strategies, professional development, and fostering a positive school culture.

Furthermore, ensuring equitable student accessibility, developing safety protocols, understanding parental engagement, and navigating regulatory compliance are merely the tip of a vast iceberg
of necessary competencies. In essence, while we anchor our faith
firmly in God's faithfulness to resource our purpose and assignments, we are simultaneously called to embrace the rigorous discipline of pursuing learning. This symbiotic relationship ensures
that we not only complete our God-given assignment but do so
with such excellence and responsibility that will truly glorify God,
demonstrating our diligent stewardship of both the vision and the
means provided.

I have invested countless hours in prayer, Bible study, fasting,
and operating in my purpose, completing God-given assignments,
and more. Yet, despite all of this, I find myself relentlessly pursuing
further knowledge, deeper wisdom, and greater understanding. For
instance, God graciously bestowed upon me the gift of teaching. As
a steward of the gift He has given me, I have consciously and wholeheartedly committed myself to a lifetime of continuous learning
that goes beyond academia. It is a sacred vow to hone my craft, to
advance in learning relentlessly, and to expand my comprehension,
all with the goal of becoming the most effective, impactful, and excellent teacher I can possibly be by truly maximizing the potential
of this precious gift.

Indeed, the very essence of effective teaching is predicated upon
an enduring spirit of studentship. How, I ask rhetorically, can one

truly impart knowledge, insight, or guidance without first being a diligent student oneself? Therefore, I earnestly implore and encourage you to embrace the practice of committing yourself unreservedly to being a lifetime learner. Respectfully, ignorance is destructive, as it is a willful rejection of trust. Deliberately pursue learning, beyond intellectual exercises, to prevent stagnation, immaturity, and stunting of your growth. God desires you to remain relevant and fully equipped to fulfill your highest calling.

No one in the Bible who was utilized by God was provided everything without work. Yes, God provides us the tools and resources we need to complete assignments, but He also requires us to put our hands to the plow and complete our assigned tasks. God recognizes that you were born for a purpose that had a pre-ordination. However, He needs human vessels like you and I to execute His assignment desires in the earth.

Noah's faith astonishes me. Consider the extraordinary context: according to Genesis 2:5-6, the earth had never known rainfall; instead, a mist rose from the ground to water the land. Yet, into this world, God spoke a seemingly impossible command to Noah: build a giant ark, a colossal vessel designed to float, and gather all species of animals within it, for a deluge unlike anything ever conceived was coming. It was going to rain.

The audacity of Noah's obedience is astonishing. He had no frame of reference for rain, let alone a global flood. While God miraculously orchestrated the animals to flock to Noah and present themselves for boarding, Noah still bore the monumental responsibility of completing his assignment: constructing the ark. Can you imagine the decades of unyielding persistence Noah must have exhibited, every strike of the hammer, every tree felled, every joint sealed, all while building a ship on dry land, with no visible threat of water? He had never seen a single drop of rain. Yet his faith in God was absolute. He believed in the coming downpour and trusted that God would provide everything needed to build a great vessel. He also believed that God would supply what was necessary to sustain and preserve life within it. His faith stretched beyond the construction; it encompassed the unseen future of survival and sustenance.

Similarly, King Solomon, renowned for the wisdom God bestowed upon him, is also celebrated for the magnificent Temple he built. God purposed Solomon to construct His sacred dwelling place, a feat of architectural and spiritual significance, and provided an influx of wealth, skilled craftsmen, and materials necessary for its erection. In fact, his father, King David, had diligently prepared for this project, amassing vast quantities of gold, silver, bronze, cedar, and other precious resources, and even drawing up detailed plans. Yet, despite this incredible head start and divine provision, it remained Solomon's direct responsibility to oversee, manage, and build the Temple. He had to orchestrate thousands of laborers, manage complex logistics, and ensure the flawless execution of God's blueprints.

The resounding principle emerging from both Noah and King Solomon is a vital lesson for us: cultivate your assignment. Do not expect God to hand you the completed vision or do the work for you. God unfailingly provides the tools, the resources, the opportunities, the wisdom, and the strength you need to fulfill your assignment. However, He expects you to pick up those tools, manage those resources, diligently labor, persist through challenges, and actively build what He has called you to create or accomplish. Our "ark" or "temple" might be a career, a family, a ministry, something personal, or a societal contribution, but in any case, God's orchestration works in tandem with human diligence. The completion of your assignment will hinge on your faithful cultivation of the assignment He has placed before you, actively using what He has provided to bring His vision to fruition.

God gave me an assignment to build a children's program at a local organization. I was excited, yet reluctant, as building without a foundation can be tedious. The funding provided was insufficient relative to the number of children I was expected to serve. The Holy Spirit began to download innovative ideas into my spirit, many of which required tools and resources I already had. Not once did I complain about the lack of resources or tools, nor did I offer my flesh the opportunity to doubt my appointed assignment.

What an honor it is to receive an assignment from the Lord! May this be your heart posture. There's a level of trust God must have in you to place an assignment in your hand. Knowing God trusted me to build a children's program consistently humbles me. In my humble perspective, God's trust is more valuable to me than anything in this world. My value of God's trust led me to build the children's program effectively with the tools and resources God provided. Now, it is your turn. Write, pray, cultivate and repeat. God has amazing things in store for you.

Affirmation to Declare Over Your Life
I will fear the Lord, for the fear of the Lord is the beginning of wisdom, and I will humbly ask Him for understanding, trusting His promise to give generously through the Holy Spirit who teaches and guides me (Prov. 1:7; Jas. 1:5; John 14:26). I choose to grow daily in the grace and knowledge of Jesus, walking in His divine direction and cultivating wisdom that bears fruit for my God-given purpose (2 Pet. 3:18; Isa. 30:21; Eph. 5:15–17).

CHAPTER SEVEN

Humility for Exaltation in Your Purpose

There must be a humility that resides in your soul, causing you to submit to God. Humility is more than an outward expression. It is an inward positioning that causes submission to God. Humility is releasing pride and surrendering the control we think we possess, choosing instead to place our lives fully in the hands of our Creator. The Bible is full of men and women who humbled themselves before God, which bred submission to His desire.

Submission to God requires your entire being. God wants all of you. When you truly understand submission, you understand that your life, agenda, time, mind, will, emotions, character, and everything belongs to God at His disposal.

Have you ever accepted a gift without knowing its origin? I have. I have four amazing children, each are uniquely designed by God, full of zeal, passion, and energy. Each time I became a mother, I surrendered my body to the design of an incubator to carry each child. Humility caused me to reconsider my entire lifestyle for the sake of the health and wellness of my children.

Humility and submission breed radical obedience. Radical obedience births purpose in your life. Submission is a lifelong task that requires consistent yield to allow God authority over your life.

Once you find your purpose, you find that assignments and destiny require continual submission.

The Journey of Exaltation

Have you ever cried out in anguish, "How could a loving God allow me to go through this?" I confess, I have, countless times. For a long time, trials, tribulations, challenges, and hardships felt like senseless burdens, impossible to understand. It was not until I consciously stepped into my God-given purpose that the true meaning of these experiences began to dawn on me. Reflecting on it, it is awe-inspiring to see how God, in His infinite wisdom, knew I possessed the strength to endure past pain and suffering. He orchestrated circumstances, not to punish, but to painstakingly fashion me into the person He desired me to be, perfectly suited for the unique purpose He crafted specifically for me. My past, marked by trials, humbled me, creating space for God to be exalted in my present and future. It was in the depths of those experiences that I began to truly understand the transformative power of perseverance.

When we consider Joseph's difficult journey to Egypt and the cascade of hurtful situations he endured, we can only conclude that he was strong enough to persevere and that his journey, despite its pain, was essential for reaching his ultimate destination. Remember, Joseph's father, Jacob, favored Joseph greatly, a fact made visually apparent by Jacob's gift of a coat of many colors. Joseph's coat showed Jacob's preferential treatment, which fueled jealousy among his brothers.

Jacob innocently sent Joseph to a nearby city to check on his flocks and, more importantly, on his brothers. Unbeknownst to Jacob, this simple errand would be the catalyst for years of suffering and separation. On his way, Joseph learned that his brothers had moved to another city, and out of selflessness, he began the arduous journey to find them. His brothers, however, saw him coming and, consumed by envy and hatred, plotted to murder him. Reuben, Joseph's oldest brother, with a flicker of conscience, intervened, derailing the murder plan and suggesting they sell him into slavery instead.

Upon Joseph's unsuspecting arrival in Dothan, his brothers seized him, stripped him of his cherished coat, and temporarily threw him into a pit, a dark foreshadowing of the trials to come. Ultimately, they coldheartedly sold Joseph into slavery, a betrayal that would forever alter the course of his life. To further cover their tracks, Joseph's brothers dipped his coat in animal blood, creating a gruesome illusion of his death, and presented it to their father, Jacob, proclaiming the tragic loss of his beloved son. Imagine the devastation Jacob must have felt, completely unaware of the treachery that had transpired.

Later, Joseph was unjustly imprisoned in Egypt. Yet, even in the depths of confinement, his God-given gift to interpret dreams shone brightly, leading him to receive favor from Pharaoh himself. His extraordinary ability catapulted him into a position of immense power, making him second in command to the Pharaoh, where he effectively governed all of Egypt.

Years later, a severe famine struck the land, forcing Joseph's family to travel to Egypt in search of sustenance. There, they found refuge and provision, and their family began to flourish. It was in Egypt that Joseph's family dwelt until after the captivity. Approximately 70 Hebrews initially entered Egypt, and over 400,000 of them exited Egypt to journey to the promised land.

Can you even begin to imagine Joseph's mental and emotional state throughout this ordeal? What if Joseph, consumed by bitterness and despair, had lost faith in God while languishing in prison? What if Joseph, hardened by his experiences, had denied his family residence in Egypt, condemning them to starvation and potential death? Where would the nation of Israel be today?

The point here is that, regardless of the seemingly insurmountable obstacles we face, we must not become self-absorbed, viewing circumstances solely as purely negative, nor should we unjustly accuse God of the heartache we experience. Instead, we are instructed to "consider it pure joy, my brothers and sisters, whenever you face trials of many kinds, because you know that the testing of your faith produces perseverance. Let perseverance finish its work so that you may be mature and complete, not lacking anything" (Jas. 1:1-4 NIV). This is not a call to feign happiness in the face of suffering, but rather a call to shift our perspective, recognizing that these trials are opportunities for growth, refinement, and ultimately, deeper intimacy with God.

Before God can exalt you, He must first purge and refine you, meticulously chiseling away the imperfections and impurities that would otherwise tarnish His name when you are elevated. You were created to have dominion in the earth. Primarily, you must have dominion over yourself. So, you need to have your faith tested, not for God's benefit (He already knows your level of faith), but for your own. It is through these tests that we cultivate perseverance and the ability to stand firm in our faith, even in the face of unimaginable challenges. Have you allowed God to test and try your faith? Are you willing to embrace these tests, recognizing their potential for growth, or are you content to remain in a state of irresolution, stagnant and unchanged?

Indeed, Joseph's faith was not only tested and tried, but proven true. The successful passage through his trials produced perseverance.

From the testing of Joseph's faith, it is evident that Joseph possessed a firm determination to serve the Lord, despite the personal cost. We can confidently conclude that God trusted Joseph to bear His name with honor and to lead His people to a new home, paving the way for the fulfillment of His covenant concerning the Promised Land.

The journey from Egypt to Canaan (the Promised Land) should have taken approximately eleven days. Yet, the Israelites spent a staggering 40 years wandering in circles in the wilderness. Why? God was meticulously trying to bring the Hebrews to a place of humility and full surrender to Him. A spiritual transformation was necessary for them to receive and to steward the blessings of the Promised Land in a way that would bring Him glory. By repeatedly worshipping other deities while in the wilderness, the Hebrews continuously rejected God demonstrating that they lacked a heart of perseverance, choosing fleeting gratification over lasting faithfulness.

While God is taking you through your own "wilderness experience," I want to encourage you to cultivate patience, choose to "count it all joy," and refuse to lose hope. Please understand that He is the God of the wilderness; He is present with you throughout your struggles, providing guidance, strength, and love.

As you are in the wilderness, it is imperative to yield to the design of the Maker. In this season, you cannot afford to allow your feelings to overtake you. Although the wilderness experience can seem frightening, rest assured that when you place your life in His hands, fear cannot demobilize you. Rest in this space. Do not allow fear of the wilderness to demobilize you. If you allow fear to overtake you, you can miss opportunities that God has predestined for you. Fear has the potential to withhold our destiny. It is a risk we cannot afford.

Before Jesus, the ultimate example of perseverance, was exalted, even He was subjected to intense testing. The famous story of

His unwavering decline of Satan's temptations in the wilderness is often paired with the message for us to speak God's Word when Satan attempts to tempt or try us, which is undoubtedly a necessity. However, please understand there is a crucial heart posture and a conditioned mindset that preceded Jesus' masterful usage of God's Word. Jesus understood the profound weight and power of God's words, recognizing their inherent ability to overrule personal desires and overcome demonic temptation. Obviously, Jesus' desire to persevere in His purpose, to fulfill His divine mission, was far more important to Him than anything the devil could possibly offer.

The humility Jesus presented in His wilderness experience is precisely what we need today. It is a conscious and deliberate rejection of what the devil, the world, or the alluring temptations of life have to offer, to completely surrender to God and humbly accept His way. It is cultivating a posture of humility so that you can be exalted in due time, according to God's perfect timing and plan. Posture your heart accordingly to God's will so you, too, can resist temptation, be tried, and persevere.

Jesus was tried and tested countless times, not only in the wilderness but also by the scribes, Pharisees, Sadducees, chief priests, and elders. Yet, He remained steadfastly faithful to God, even in the face of relentless opposition. God was able to take Jesus from faith to faith and glory to glory (Rom. 1:17) because of His unwavering perseverance. As His faith was tested and refined, He developed an even stronger resolve until His final, sacrificial act of love on the cross.

We readily celebrate the triumphant stories of Joseph rising from the pit to the palace, and of Jesus' ascent from the manger to the right-hand of God's throne. Yet we often detest the arduous journey of humility, the necessary process of refinement that precedes a breakthrough. Often, our underlying issue is a lack of patience; we are obsessed with being exalted and feeling successful, neglecting the patient work of inner transformation. I pray you grow to a place where you realize that your fleeting feelings should never take precedence over God's unwavering desire to chisel away all your mess and to refine you into a vessel that is clean, pure, and perfectly prepared for your God-given purpose. Only then can you truly experience the fullness of His blessings and the profound joy of living a life that glorifies Him.

Prayer Points and Scriptures to Pray

Humility So God Can Exalt You:
James 4:10 NIV—"Humble yourselves before the Lord, and he will lift you up."

Understanding that God is the Lifter of Men:
1 Peter 5:6 (NIV)—"Humble yourselves, therefore, under God's mighty hand, that he may lift you up in due time."

Patience in Tribulation:
Romans 12:12 (NIV)—"Be joyful in hope, patient in affliction, faithful in prayer."

Grace as God Prunes You for Exaltation:
John 15:1-2 (NIV)—"I am the true vine, and my Father is the gardener. He cuts off every branch in me that bears no fruit, while every branch that does bear fruit he prunes[a] so that it will be even more fruitful."

Acceptance of Whatever Season God has You In:
Psalm 31:14-15 (NIV)—"But I trust in you, Lord; I say, 'You are my God.' My times are in your hands; deliver me from the hands of my enemies, from those who pursue me."

Affirmation to Declare Over Your Life
I humble myself under the mighty hand of God, trusting that in His perfect time He will lift me up, and I choose to be joyful in hope, patient in affliction, and faithful in prayer as He refines me for His purpose (Jas. 4:10; 1 Pet. 5:6; Rom. 12:12). I welcome the Father's pruning and declare with confidence that my times are in His hands, knowing that every season—whether hidden preparation or breakthrough—secures my destiny and exalts me for His glory (John 15:1–2; Psalm 31:14–15).

CHAPTER EIGHT

Measuring Success in Your Purpose

The conventional world often equates success with tangible achievements: a hefty bank account, a luxury car, a beautiful house. These materialistic measures, however, are a shallow and ultimately immature understanding of what it truly means to be successful. True success transcends the external and resides within the spirit, stemming from a life surrendered to God and subsequently manifesting outwardly in positive ways. Many individuals may be named successful in earthly terms, and tragically do not rise to God's standard, facing eternal separation from Him. As Jesus eloquently declared, "For what is a man profited, if he shall gain the whole world, and lose his own soul? Or what shall a man give in exchange for his soul?" (Matt. 16:26 KJV). Such questions compel us to re-evaluate our priorities and definitions of success.

Our soul, the very essence of our being, encompasses our mind, will, and emotions. Therefore, true success lies in soul prosperity: a state of holistic well-being where our thoughts, desires, and feelings align and operate in God's will and desire. Soul prosperity is achieved through the conscious act of self-denial, a deliberate relinquishing of our own ego-driven impulses in favor of embracing the mind, will, and emotions of God. Jesus Christ exemplified this principle; His soul prospered, enabling Him to successfully fulfill His divine purpose and assignments, launching Him into His destiny through self-denial.

The narrative in Matthew 16 provides a powerful illustration of this concept. Following the pivotal declaration of Jesus as the Messiah, the Son of God, through Peter's revelatory proclamation, Jesus foretold His impending suffering, death, and resurrection. Peter, deeply concerned and clinging to a humanistic perspective, rebuked Jesus, exclaiming, "Be it far from thee, Lord: this shall not be unto thee" (Matt. 16:22 KJV). Jesus' sharp rebuke to Peter, "Get thee behind me, Satan: thou art an offence unto me: for thou savourest not the things that be of God, but those that be of men" (Matt. 16:23 KJV), exemplifies the stark contrast between earthly desires and God's design.

In this pivotal moment, we witness Jesus accepting God's will for His life. He was purposed to be the Savior of the world, a mission that required His sacrifice on the cross. Jesus embraced His destiny, understanding the purpose behind His birth. Furthermore, Jesus not only accepted His own path but also provided His disciples, and by extension us, the formula for true success: "If any man will come after me, let him deny himself, and take up his cross, and follow me. For whosoever will save his life shall lose it: and whosoever will lose his life for my sake shall find it" (Matt.16:24-25 KJV). This is not a call to physical suffering but a metaphor for surrendering our self-centered desires and embracing God's plan.

Denying oneself is not a passive act but an active and ongoing process of purging and pruning. It requires a continual effort to eliminate aspects of our lives that hinder true intimacy with God. It demands full submission to His will, a conscious choice to die to the flesh, to suppress our selfish inclinations, and to embrace humility. When we deny ourselves, we begin to depend on God, recognizing that He is the vine and we are the branches. A branch cannot thrive independently; it requires constant connection to the vine, the source of its life, nourishment, and vitality. The vine provides the necessary oxygen, minerals, and vitamins for the branch's survival and growth. Similarly, when we deny our own limited mind, self-serving will, and fleeting emotions, and take up our cross (symbolizing sacrifice and commitment), we become a branch intrinsically connected to the Tree of Life, receiving sustenance and purpose, assignments, and destiny from God.

Clinging to our limited understanding of life and stubbornly holding onto self-centered desires will ultimately lead to profound loss. To experience true success, we must willingly surrender our lives, our preconceived notions, and our individual ambitions, so that we can receive His abundant and purposeful life in return. Jesus' message in Matthew 16:24-25 is a clear warning: our default, innate inclinations will lead to eternal death. True life, and therefore true success, is found only in Him. The life we discover in Him offers an accelerated path toward pleasing God and fulfilling His purpose for us. It is achieved through the rejection of our ungodly desires, fleeting sentiments, and distorted thought processes, and embracing His perfect and eternal truth. Ultimately, true success is not about what we accumulate but about who we become in Christ.

The Vine & Branch

The spring air hummed with my burgeoning enthusiasm as I embarked on a new, vibrant adventure: growing my very own garden. With a heart brimming with optimistic ambition, I spent hours poring over online catalogs, delightedly selecting a diverse array of fruit and vegetable seeds, each promising a bountiful harvest.

My excitement spilled over into several spirited store runs, where I meticulously gathered all the essentials: nutrient-rich soil, sturdy gardening tools, and an assortment of miscellaneous items. I truly believed, with an unshakeable conviction born of a "gardener's heart," that my backyard oasis would soon transform into the largest, healthiest, and most flourishing garden in the neighborhood: a testament to my green thumb.

Long story, incredibly short, the reality was a stark contrast to my verdant dreams. After weeks and weeks of eager anticipation, watering, and hopeful peering at the barren soil, a single, solitary head of lettuce emerged, a rather pathetic symbol of my initial endeavors. Disheartened but not defeated, my determination ignited anew. Refusing to be deterred by this meager yield, I resolved to try again. This time, I planted an even more ambitious spread: about twenty different types of fruits and vegetables. To my astonishment, every single seed sprouted with remarkable vigor!

However, my second attempt brought forth a new challenge. With my children joining in the newfound excitement, we diligently followed online tutorials on how to nurture a garden, eagerly discussing sunlight, soil, and growth. Yet, in our overzealousness, we inadvertently committed a cardinal gardening sin: over-watering. Our well-intentioned care became a deluge, effectively drowning the delicate seeds before they had a chance to take root. To compound the problem, the chosen environment itself proved less than ideal, perhaps lacking adequate sunlight or proper drainage, ultimately hindering the potential for growth.

Moving from the literal to the spiritual, this gardening narrative serves as a poignant analogy for measuring success in the Kingdom of God. Our ultimate pursuit is to bear fruit that remains (John 15:16), not fleeting achievements, but lasting impact with eternal significance. To achieve this, we are called to intimately connect with and glean from the very character of Christ, who is the True Vine, and we, His disciples, are the branches. The inherent duty of every branch is to produce fruit, drawing its very lifeblood and nourishment directly from the Vine. This symbiotic relationship underscores God's truth: a branch cannot produce fruit, nor can it even survive, if it is severed or absent from the Vine. Conversely, the fruit itself cannot exist apart from the branch or the Vine. This message of dependence, purpose, and life is precisely what Jesus conveyed in John 15:1-8.

Indeed, the concept of fruitfulness is not new to God's grand design. In the very beginning, God commanded man and woman to "be fruitful, and multiply, and replenish the earth" (Gen. 1:28). God's inaugural mandate for humanity set the stage for purpose and destiny. Now, thousands of years later, Jesus, through the powerful imagery of the vine and branches, is expounding on the spiritual implications of fruitfulness, multiplication, and replenishment in John 15. The recurrence and emphasis of this theme throughout scripture unequivocally attest to the paramount importance of productivity, growth, and maturation in God's eternal design!

When you faithfully bear fruit, our loving and wise God will prune you to refine you. Pruning involves carefully removing anything that might hinder increased fruit production. Pruning can be a painful and uncomfortable process. However, please view it as an essential process for your growth and greater spiritual yield.

The absolute prerequisite for bearing any fruit is to abide in Jesus, for as He plainly states in John 15:5 (NIV), "apart from me you can do nothing." You literally cannot bear lasting, spiritual fruit without His constant presence and power in your life. You must abide in Him. It is God who "gives seed to the sower" (2 Cor. 9:10), equipping us with gifts, talents, resources, tools, and opportunities. How we utilize these seeds, how faithfully we sow them into His Kingdom, and the fruit that results from that sowing together determine how we measure true success in the Kingdom of God.

When fruit is removed from its source, whether a tree, vine, or plant, it immediately begins the gradual process of decay and death. It wilts, shrivels, and eventually perishes. Now, imagine a radical counter-concept: what if I told you that when you bear fruit in the Spirit, it does not die? It is not mere poetic license; it is reality.

Please understand, the eternal Source from which your spiritual fruit originates, God Himself, cannot and will never die. Thus, when you bear fruit in the Spirit, abiding in Christ, that fruit carries eternal quality—it remains. It will literally never perish, as long as God's prerequisites of connection, obedience, and nourishment through abiding in Jesus remain intact. This fruit has lasting value, impacting lives for eternity.

This brings us to a series of introspective questions: What have you done with the precious seeds God has entrusted to your care: your unique gifts, talents, time, tools, resources, etc.? Have your seeds been diligently planted in fertile ground, or are they lying dormant, perhaps even buried? Do you cultivate a heart and spirit that demonstrate capacity, a readiness to receive and steward more seeds from God? How much spiritual fruit have you borne, and what is its lasting impact? Most importantly, are you consistently and actively abiding in Christ: the only sustainable, life-giving Vine?

We often look for instant breakthroughs and growth, but even the most amazing ministries had humble, gradual beginnings. Jesus, the Messiah Himself, did not begin healing the sick, raising the dead, preaching with power and authority, and teaching with wisdom the mysteries of God the moment He exited Mary's womb. There was a deliberate and gradual progression in His ministry.

We can only imagine the sleepless nights Jesus spent in fervent prayer and the weariness He experienced from long journeys and physical weakness during seasons of fasting. He felt frustration over the spiritual blindness of the Pharisees and Sadducees. He also knew the deep sadness of seeing humanity as "sheep without a shepherd," both before and throughout His earthly ministry.

I am absolutely convinced that Jesus spent countless hours stowed away in intentional prayer. He practiced dedicated fasting and the study of the scriptures, all to meticulously prepare, cultivate, and align Himself perfectly with the purpose, assignments, and destiny of His life. His eventual public ministry was the culmination of years of spiritual growth and preparation.

Oftentimes, folks reference Paul's (formerly Saul's) dramatic conversion on the road to Damascus and become excited, assuming God elevated him to prominence in ministry almost instantaneously. Please understand that before Paul's transformative encounter with Christ, he was not an uneducated, "unchurched" individual. He was a highly educated and a devout Pharisee, a rigorous sect that meticulously served God, characterized by intense discipline, consecration, and zealous adherence to the Mosaic Law.

Paul was fully engrossed in understanding and upholding the Law. Therefore, while conversion to Christianity was undeniably a monumental leap of faith and a radical redirection of his life, many of the foundational components of spiritual discipline, intellectual rigor, and commitment, Paul already possessed. Even he, despite the dramatic nature of his conversion, experienced a period of gradual growth and preparation, though scripture does not always provide every intimate detail.

It is important, however, to understand that Paul began preaching relatively shortly after his conversion. Scripture explicitly states that he "increased the more in strength" (Acts 9:22 KJV) because he was actively bearing fruit. So, while it may appear as if, as soon as he was converted and experienced an immediate, non-gradual elevation, please understand that he certainly had a process of gradual spiritual growth and refinement that may have involved God quickly accelerating his ministry forward precisely because of his diligence, his prepared heart, and the abundant fruit that he was bearing. God's acceleration is often a reward for faithful preparation, stewardship, and obedience.

As Ecclesiastes 7:8 (KJV) wisely states, "Better is the end of a thing than the beginning thereof." Your conclusion, the summation of your life's journey, is undeniably more important and impactful than your initial starting point. At the end of your life, everything about you will be remembered. Your words, deeds, conduct, and character will be revealed and evaluated. This may happen at your funeral or in the quiet reflections of those whose lives you have touched.

The day you entered this world as a precious package fully equipped to launch into your unique purpose, was undoubtedly a wonderful event. However, it pales in comparison to the collective weight and consequence of the days, months, years, and decades you will spend actively walking, growing, and bearing fruit in your God-given purpose. It is the journey, the transformation, and the lasting impact that can truly define your success in your purpose, assignments, and destiny. May God receive all the glory for what He will accomplish in the earth through you.

Prayer Points & Scriptures to Pray

Your Success is Defined by Your Flourishing in God:

Psalm 1:1-3 (NIV)—"Blessed is the one who does not walk in step with the wicked or stand in the way that sinners take or sit in the company of mockers, but whose delight is in the law of the LORD, and who meditates on his law, day and night. That person is like a tree planted by streams of water, which yields its fruit in season and whose leaf does not wither—whatever they do prospers."

You Bear Fruit that Remains:

John 15:16 (NIV)—"You did not choose me, but I chose you and appointed you so that you might go and bear fruit—fruit that will last—and so that whatever you ask in my name the Father will give you."

Persevering in Your Relationship with God Beyond Financial Gain

Deuteronomy 6:5 (NIV)—"Love the Lord your God with all your heart and with all your soul and with all your strength."

Alignment with God's Desire:

Psalm 37:4 (NIV)—"Take delight in the Lord, and he will give you the desires of your heart."

Your Soul Prospers and You are Healthy:

3 John 1:2 (NIV)—"Dear friend, I pray that you may enjoy good health and that all may go well with you, even as your soul is getting along well."

Affirmation to Declare Over Your Life

I am chosen and planted by God to flourish in His purpose, bearing fruit that remains and prospers in season (Psalm 1:1–3; John 15:16). As I delight in the Lord and love Him with all my heart, soul, and strength, my soul thrives and my purpose aligns with His perfect will (Deuteronomy 6:5; Psalm 37:4; 3 John 1:2).

Afterword

I pray this book provides you guidance, wisdom, understanding, and direction. With a heart overflowing with fervent hope and expectation, I intercede in prayer for you, dear reader.

Abba Father, in the matchless name of Your beloved Son, Yeshua, our Lord and Savior, I come before You on behalf of the reader of this book. With reverence and a spirit of humility, yet with the boldness instilled by the precious shed blood of Yeshua, I come before Your glorious throne of grace, recognizing Your infinite majesty. I come confident that, in Your presence, we shall indeed obtain mercy and find help in the time of need, according to Your Word in Hebrews 4:16.

My heart swells with gratitude as I acknowledge and give thanks that You, the Master Artisan, have uniquely woven each of us into being, fearfully and wonderfully made, bearing Your image, as declared in Psalms 139:14. Each life is a masterpiece, a testament to Your creative genius. I thank You, Lord, for planting within the reader's heart a deep, unyielding yearning and hunger to truly comprehend and embrace their unique purpose, the specific assignments You have strategically prepared for them, and the glorious destiny You have ordained before the foundation of the world.

Therefore, I earnestly implore You, Holy Spirit, to lead the reader with undeniable clarity and unerring precision into all truth. May Your truth, unadulterated and pure, illuminate their path and reveal the mysteries of God. I speak divine protection over them and their entire household. Please draw a supernatural cordon of safety around them. Cover them, Father, with the precious blood of

Yeshua, establishing an impenetrable shield against all harm, sickness, and the snares of the enemy.

Graciously bestow upon them, O Lord, your guidance that leaves no room for doubt. Give them understanding to discern Your ways, supernatural wisdom to navigate complexities, and an unshakeable inner strength rooted in Your power. Enable them to steadfastly complete every assignment, fully realize their God-given purpose, and majestically walk into the fullness of their predestined destiny.

Now, by the inherent, unyielding power and absolute authority established through the victorious, shed blood of Yeshua, I rise in intercession. I rebuke, disarm, and dismantle every demonic attack, every assignment of darkness, and oppressive stronghold that dares to rise against their destiny, their calling, their health, their relationships, and Your provision. I declare them null and void, by the blood of Yeshua! Furthermore, I boldly call upon the mighty, ministering angels of the Lord, Your heavenly hosts, to encamp around them, to lift them, guard them in all their ways, and actively minister to their every need, seen and unseen.

As You, in Your infinite provision, begin to strategically bring forth and unveil the necessary tools, divine connections, financial resources, spiritual gifts, opportunities, and insights tailored for the advancement of their God-given purpose and assignments, I pray that they will possess a spirit of wise stewardship. May they never squander or misuse such precious provisions, but rather employ all resources with intention, integrity, and utmost dedication. May every resource be leveraged strategically and effectively, not for personal gain or fleeting acclaim, but solely and entirely for Your eternal glory and the expansion of Your Kingdom.

Know they bear the sacred, hallowed name of Yeshua: the name above all names, Your beloved Son and ambassador on earth. I pray for a fervent desire within every reader to continually seek Your face, to know Your heart, and to comprehend the desire and will of God on every matter. May they passionately pursue Your abiding presence, the tangible, transformative anointing, and manifest power of the Holy Spirit in every facet of their life.

May every thought in their mind be captive to Christ, and Your righteousness guide every action. May their public and private life reflect Your holiness. Let every part of their character be a living testament to Your image. May their entire being be seamlessly and perfectly aligned with Your infallible Word, sovereign will, righteous desire, and perfect way, bringing honor and glory to Your name in all things.

When the inevitable but necessary season of pruning comes to refine and strip away all that hinders fruitfulness and growth, I pray, Father, that the challenging encounters of pain, righteous chastisement, or unsettling confusion will not lead to despair. Instead, may they be permeated by Your tender comfort, love, and the gentle reassurance of Your abiding presence, knowing that Your pruning is always rooted in love.

Above all, through every triumph and trial, every mountaintop and valley, I pray with all my heart that the reader would always, without a single shadow of a doubt, know and experience Your unconditional and everlasting love and care.

Thank you, Lord. In Yeshua's name, amen and amen!

Connect and Share

Thank you for reading *Praying Into Your Purpose*. If you enjoyed this book, please leave a review on Amazon and the website where you purchased it.

Connect with Author Andrea Jackson online:

Website:
https://www.royaltylifecoach.com/

Instagram:
@confidence_supportgroup

Facebook:
https://www.facebook.com/share/1U6kXrcMG6/

www.ingramcontent.com/pod-product-compliance
Lightning Source LLC
Chambersburg PA
CBHW051548120626
46551CB00013B/1419